Praise for *The Design Thinking Classroom*

"I love how this book emphasizes ON THE FIRST PAGE that our students should be active, engaged participants in their communities. Deeper, hands-on learning experiences for schoolchildren don't happen by magic or with wishful thinking. This book is an extremely helpful guide for how to design these high-agency, high-impact learning activities. The book includes a strong emphasis on educator mindset and capacity-building and is full of practical scenarios and examples. I can't recommend this book highly enough for educators who want to transform their traditional classrooms into design studios and make school different."

> **—Dr. Scott McLeod,** professor of educational leadership, University of Colorado Denver, and founding director, CASTLE

"In *The Design Thinking Classroom*, David Jakes provides a clear and articulate path beyond the current form of public P–16 education as a culture of compliance and discipline to a progressive pedagogical approach that is agile, responsive, and supportive of student needs. With insightful paths for developing educational experiences from a design thinking perspective, Jakes's book is a must read for educators, administrators, elected school officials, and public policy makers who truly want to gain a vision of the mindsets, values, and characteristics our public schools *should* embody. As he unwraps the educator-designer mindset, he uses lessons learned from our educational past to clearly articulate a vision for schools and classrooms of the future. In an engaging and empowering voice, Jakes counters traditional and stagnant viewpoints of P–16 education with practical opportunities for educators to enrich and improve their current practices in order to do what is right, just, and equitable for future generations of students."

> **—Jeremy S. Brueck, PhD,** assistant professor of education, University of Mount Union

"Must read! At their core, every teacher is and has been a *designer*, whether they've realized it or not. David Jakes's new book provides teachers with concrete principles for improving in their role as educator-designers, ensuring teachers are better equipped to develop the learning experiences every student deserves."

—Darren E. Draper, EdD, director of innovative learning, Alpine School District, Utah

"Lifelong learning is the cliché du jour in books on improving student outcomes. But with well over a quarter century of experience in classrooms and schools, David Jakes knows better than to speak about the hard work of school change in simple clichés. Riffing off the term in more meaningful ways, Jakes describes the need for schools to create 'life-deep learning' and 'life-wide learning' experiences. Never merely suggestive, Jakes sketches out a pathway for such learning, and it begins with a new role for the teacher: the educator-designer. Urging us to question not only our methods but also the very physical space of our classroom, Jakes carves the shape of this new educator as one that is less about efficiency and more about authenticity, less about discrete details and more about skills development like observation, inquiry, and developing points of view. Jakes's educator-designer is a bold vision of a teacher, one whose curriculum comes to life through the imposition of complex, real-world problems between the students and their nascent understanding of the world. Never simple or naive, Jakes's book asks all of us involved in the work of education what we believe about how our children learn best, whether our current systems are designed to meet those beliefs, and what we can do when they are not."

—Garreth Heidt, English teacher and co-creator of Perkiomen Valley's Social Entrepreneurship and Innovation class, NOVA Lab: A Space for Inspiration, Aspiration, Respiration, and Creation

"David Jakes is a thoughtful educator reflecting on a lifelong career in educational spaces. Using his own personal evolution as the foundation for this book, Jakes provides the reader with a wide range of lenses, strategies, and tools for implementing a design-based pedagogy with insightful questions and limitless possibilities. At its core, Jakes has written a book that implores education to be infinitely more human and humane, centering people in the design of their own learning and spaces."

—**Diana Laufenberg,** executive director Inquiry Schools, Inc.

"This is a deeply heartful, human-centric and useful book that is an important read for everyone from that teacher who is just beginning their journey to a design-thinking classroom to the educator experienced in co-creation of learning who is looking to sharpen their skills and refresh their thinking. David uses his own journey as an educator to frame how design thinking can create schools that are more thoughtful, passionate and powerful places for us all."

—**Chris Lehmann,** founding principal and CEO, Science Leadership Academy Schools, Philadelphia, Pennsylvania

"As we exit one of the most difficult times in the history of education, David Jakes presents us with a provocation to truly change our educational systems for the better. Not only does this book push school officials to reflect and think deeper into the future, but also provides skills and examples on how to achieve it."

—**Glenn Robbins,** superintendent, Brigantine School District, Brigantine, New Jersey

"David Jakes's insightful and practical book is a hope-filled, well-lit pathway for educators on the threshold of giving up or giving in. With a designer's perspective and some new skills, we can reimagine life-wide and life-deep learning with our students and make good on our promise to help them launch lives of purpose and impact. We might well find it again for ourselves in the process."

—**Laura Walker Deisley,** managing consultant, Walker Deisley Strategic Consulting, LLC, and founder, Lab Atlanta, Inc.

The Design Thinking Classroom

THE
Design
Thinking
CLASSROOM

USING DESIGN THINKING TO REIMAGINE
THE ROLE AND PRACTICE OF EDUCATORS

DAVID JAKES

This book is available at special discounts when purchased in quantity for educational purposes or for use as premiums, promotions, or fundraisers. For inquiries and details, contact the publisher at books@impressbooks.org.

Published by IMPress, a division of Dave Burgess Consulting, Inc.
IMPressbooks.org
DaveBurgessConsulting.com
San Diego, CA

Library of Congress Control Number: 2022949581
Paperback ISBN: 978-1-948334-62-4
Ebook ISBN: 978-1-948334-63-1

Cover and interior design by Liz Schreiter
Edited and produced by Reading List Editorial
ReadingListEditorial.com

CONTENTS

CHAPTER 1

Understanding the Design Thinking Process

There are timeless qualities that contribute to the success of an educator:

Openness and honesty with students.

Preparedness—and showing up with it every day.

Respect for kids and a commitment to treating them fairly.

An ability to create learning experiences that challenge and interest them.

Being a learner yourself and letting students see that.

A willingness to be involved in kids' lives and share in their successes and their failures.

It's all fairly simple. But extraordinarily challenging. Educators that exhibit these qualities collectively form the foundation of schools that serve their communities in the right way.

Likewise, there are timeless elements that contribute to a successful school experience: Students should have the opportunity to engage in learning experiences that enable them to develop the qualities of an educated person. They should learn to be part of a community and develop an understanding of what it means to be part of something larger than themselves. There should be challenges that test their growth and development—challenges that occur across a range of experiences and venues from the classroom to the homecoming dance and from the athletic field to the auditorium stage. And students must participate in experiences that enable them to develop the qualities of being human—qualities such as empathy, compassion, courage, resiliency, among others—that will serve them their entire lives.

While these elements are timeless, the ways in which students experience them at school cannot be. A world in perpetual beta declares this to be true and demands a new context for the development of the requisite knowledge, skills, and dispositions that will contribute to a life worth living. It is likely that this new context for a learning experience will need to be broader and extend beyond the physical brick-and-mortar experience of the school. This suggests that the experience of school will potentially be more connective and employ the community as well as the world as a landscape for learning. Given that, there is an opportunity to help learners develop and explore hyperindividualized pathways for learning (beyond what is now labeled as personalized learning) that help them negotiate this landscape—while at the same time enabling them to explore a wide range of experiences, passions, and interests—and, in the process, find the *launch point* for their lives.

A worthy challenge for every school is to determine what a new context for learning means to them. This undoubtedly is a question that must be answered by each school and its community. And although ideas may differ, a new context for learning ultimately requires a new and broader role for educators. It's time to add to that list of timeless qualities that contribute to the success of an educator.

This book is about the new role of *educator-designer*, a professional who has the capacity to make sense of the robust and diverse conditions available for learning today and tomorrow and who uses the design thinking process to craft a new school and classroom experience, in partnership with students, their school community, and potentially with the entire world.

THEN VS. NOW

I started teaching high school biology in 1986.

I remember walking into my first classroom, a very odd-shaped room that had a large greenhouse attached to it. I was assigned to teach two life science courses, one called Plant and Soil Science that used the greenhouse as a lab. I was quite apprehensive and intimidated: Like any first-year teacher, I had to learn everything that was required of an educator, but I had to do that while running a full-scale greenhouse operation. That was made even more intimidating because my major in college was *aquatic* biology!

I recall asking my department chair if there were curricula for the two courses. He said that there wasn't, but there was a collection of old college textbooks in the closet that I could use to figure out what to teach. More apprehension. And stress.

So in my first year in education, I was teaching five sections of science with no curriculum, very limited and outdated resources, and of course, very limited teaching experience. My odd-shaped classroom, with its old desks bolted to the floor, a teacher desk, battleship-gray filing cabinet, and wall of cabinets, didn't help. And let's not forget the chalkboard that certainly had seen better days. The room also included a screen and an overhead projector—that was destined to become one of my best friends. The only other technology that I had was a garage-sale slide projector I'd picked up. There were no copy machines available in the school, only ditto machines. If I was lucky, I could get several of my colleagues to help me lift and carry a 16 mm film projector to my room, which was between floor levels and had no access to it other than stairs.

Admittedly, the educational experience in my classes was dominated by direct instruction, though there were occasional lab experiences and films. After a while, I branched out and began taking 35 mm slides of images in the old textbooks to use in lectures. In 1986, that required photographing the images and sending them out for development as slides—a process that could take well over a week.

That was the reality of my teaching experience in 1986. Availability of personal computers in school was years away, access to the internet at least a decade away, and the concept of the modern smartphone was pure science fiction.

Things changed in education, a greater range of educational experiences became possible, and teaching and learning in schools certainly got more interesting. Over my twenty-seven-year career in education, with fifteen of those years teaching science, I saw major changes to education. Technology arrived, first with the laser disc (no more slides!) and then computers, with the introduction of the Mac Classic, which brought new opportunities to explore creativity, including things like HyperCard programming. My school started to explore project-based learning, and there was a focus on promoting student engagement. We started to improve curricula, align coursework, and create better, shared assessments as we looked to break down departmental silos.

Compared to my situation, most beginning teachers today will have a completely different experience, except for the rigor of learning how to become a teacher. Curriculum is available on the web. Images can be located online, downloaded quickly, and assembled into a presentation during a single prep period. Connections to other teachers can be made quickly through social media to ask for advice and to share ideas. Most—if not all—students might have a laptop to connect to online resources and to each other. Books and textbooks most will likely be available on the web. And . . . students walk into the room with a computer in their pocket more powerful than the machines that put men on the moon. It doesn't stop there. Today's teacher can consider the options of project-based learning, blended and virtual learning, mastery- and competency-based learning, and challenge-based learning. There are new trends associated with making and makerspaces, STEM and STEAM, Esports, and what it means to be future ready.

There has been no other time when there is so much capacity for creating a truly unique and meaningful school learning experience for students. In fact, the opportunity is so expansive and complex, and changes so quickly, that it presents a completely new set of challenges for teachers. When I started teaching, my landscape was limited; today the opposite is true.

I began my career as the classic "sage on the stage" teacher, with moments where I became the "guide on the side." Today, teachers are often called to assume the role of facilitator, but I think that name is too limited to describe the elegance that is required to teach students and do it well. I think that teachers need a new role, one that favors an ability to negotiate the robust landscape of today's world, make the necessary connections to students in a hyperconnected world, and prepare students to find their identity, their passions, and the opportunities that will *launch their lives.*

It's time to discard the roles and identities of the past and embrace a new vision and role for today's teacher: *the educator-designer.*

To accomplish this, I'm going to encourage you to embrace the process of design thinking. As a teacher, you already design learning experiences for students while striving to create the conditions for them to develop as learners and as people. I want to help you build on that and provide you with a powerful process—along with the strategies, techniques, and tools—that will increase your design abilities. It is my hope that this will lead you to a new state of empowerment in creating new classroom experiences for you and your students.

Empowerment is a big word, and perhaps it's sometimes overused. Every teacher faces the realistic constraints of school goals and expectations, curriculum, time—and the list goes on. But despite all of this, every teacher I have ever known has wanted to get better at what they do. And that's how the design thinking process can help: leading the way to improving and becoming more innovative as a teacher while advancing the educational experience you provide your students.

FROM PRACTITIONER TO DESIGNER: MY JOURNEY

To this day, I'm still embarrassed to tell this story.

But I will, because it serves to illustrate the role design can have in reshaping how you think and approach your professional practice. That's what happened when I first got started with the process of design thinking. I had been invited to participate in a weekend design event to reimagine K–12 school libraries in Atlanta, Georgia. At the time, I was an instructional technology coordinator for a large school district in the Chicago suburbs. I'd received the invitation from two members of my extended educational network, both of whom were design professionals, and I eagerly accepted it. I was excited to develop my understanding about libraries and meet and engage interesting people from a wide range of professions in and around education. I wasn't thinking about design at all.

During the event, I attended a workshop led by a futurist, who asked, "What if there were no school libraries, what would that mean for schools and for learning?"

I immediately blurted out a response, "There will always be libraries in schools!"

Every head in the room—the speaker as well as every other workshop participant—turned and just looked at me. Silence. Finally, others started commenting and offering their thoughts about the futurist's provocation, and the event continued without anyone responding to my statement.

As you might expect, I was horrified. Throughout the event and then afterward, I reflected on my comment and the experience of the weekend. I realized that I tended to think in absolutes, and that considering new ideas and possibilities that weren't consistent with my world view of education was a challenge for me. I realized that my thinking was rigid and constrained, reflecting the traditional expectations of what school was and could be. My beliefs were based on my experience as an educator, what I knew and had experienced, and who I was. Although I considered myself to be a creative person, I realized that I was not open to truly divergent thinking and disruptive ideas. It was difficult to think beyond my practitioner's assumptions and biases. My mindset was fixed, and the lens that I saw possibilities through was limited and predictable.

That experience had a profound impact on the trajectory of my career and how I approached thinking about what was possible for the educational experience of school. Taking a cue from the others at the event, I began to dedicate myself to learning everything I could about design. And the more I learned, the more I became convinced that it could reframe the way I thought about education and how I practiced my craft. I read and tried different elements of the design process. Some things were mildly effective; most were not. Gradually, I learned the language and process of design, what might be possible, and how it might impact what I did as an educator. And I got better at thinking like a designer.

Since then, I have continually learned more about how to design. No two school engagements are exactly alike, and each presents its unique challenges and opportunities. Here's a simple analogy: Learning the design thinking process is like learning Photoshop. There is always more to learn and uncover since the tool is so capable and can be used in so many ways to accomplish such a wide variety of creative tasks. When complex problems become challenging, I always return to the design process to ground my work. And, over time, this has given me the confidence as a design professional to tackle the challenging and complex questions that I encounter.

My hope is that this book helps you apply the design thinking process to your practice and create a new direction and identity for the experience you provide students. It is also my hope that it helps you to think differently and more creatively so that you can see the possibilities in every opportunity.

AN INTRODUCTION TO DESIGN THINKING

Everything that you use daily has been designed in one way or another. Humans have been designing things to improve their lives forever.

The process of design thinking, however, is relatively new. Credit for the term itself is generally given to the international design firm IDEO, and it has become commonplace in business and industry to describe design thinking as a *human-centered and strategic process used to create solutions for people that improve the experiences of their lives.*

THE DESIGN THINKING PROCESS

So, what does the process look like?

Design thinking is typically thought of as a process in five phases:

Empathize
Define
Ideate
Prototype
Test

The phases are often depicted as sequential, but you'll soon realize that the process is iterative and that designers can enter and reenter the process at any point as needed. Accordingly, the process is flexible and malleable, and you're encouraged to think about how you can shape it to make it your own. That is exactly what I have done over the past decade.

As you might expect, people have described the design thinking process in different ways. If you do a Google image search on design thinking, you'll see a wide variety of visual representations of the process. The model of design thinking presented here reflects my experience as a public-school teacher and administrator and as a practicing designer for an international design firm based in Chicago. The terminology throughout this book and the way I explain design thinking has been heavily influenced by my experience working at that design firm and my continued work with architects. For example, in the following model, I use *discover* to represent the first phase, which I believe is a more robust description of the intent of the phase than *empathize*, which many others use. I have also included an additional phase, the Implement phase, which supports action and impact. My goal is to present what I have learned about the process and create the most understandable model that I can to help you become conversant in the design thinking methodology.

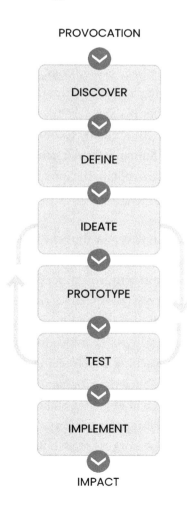

The Provocation

The design thinking process begins with a design challenge or provocation. The provocation is a general charge provided to the designers by the client that simply describes an initial design direction. For example, a provocation might be to design a new STEM center on campus or to create a new type of physical education course. The provocation articulates an interest and provides a starting point. It is the job of the designer to then begin a process with stakeholders to understand the context for the provocation by engaging in the discover process.

Discover

After the provocation has been issued, designers begin the discover phase, or *discovery*. During discovery, the designer identifies stakeholder groups who can offer insights into the provocation and engages them through a variety of ethnography techniques. The process of ethnography, or the study of human behaviors and customs, includes a set of techniques designers use to obtain the information necessary to drive the design process, like surveys, interviews with focus groups, observations, and workshops.

During discovery, designers take the time to listen, observe, and ask questions to understand everything they can about the people they are designing with. Most importantly, this process must occur without the designer interjecting their own perspectives and biases into the process. I constantly remind myself of this when I work with a school, because I spent twenty-seven years in public education and certainly have my perspectives on schools, teaching, and learning. Discovery is not a time to judge or evaluate others but a time for gaining a deep understanding.

The amount of time spent engaging stakeholders varies according to the complexity of the design opportunity. I may initially spend two days to complete discovery, working face to face on campus with a client for smaller projects. When I partner with an architecture firm to support the design of a new school, I typically spend a week on site with the architect team.

> When I worked at a design firm in Chicago, my specialty became community engagement, where my role was to support our team with planning and executing discovery. Today, in my private practice, I still consider that a significant part of my expertise. In Chapter 6, I'll share with you the tools and processes that I have developed to successfully engage stakeholders. These are available to you through my website for download so that you can leverage an entire set of tools that have been tested and work.
>
> **davidjakesdesigns.com/educatordesigner**

Define

In the define phase, designers process the information from the discover phase and look for the trends and patterns that can be used to develop a problem statement, also called the point of view (POV). This is a global statement that reflects the designer's interpretation of the insights gained from the discover phase, and it serves to frame and guide the remainder of the process. Following the development of the POV, a set of design drivers are created to provide a more detailed vision of the design opportunity. Every single design project I do with schools is based on a point-of-view statement and supported by a set of design drivers.

POV. Think of the point of view as a statement that synthesizes all that you have learned about who you are designing with, their needs, and what they want to accomplish and create.

Here are some hypothetical examples of a POV statement from the imaginary Anytown School.

How might we create a new library experience at the Anytown School based on contemporary literacy that helps students develop the skills and dispositions of an engaged citizen?

How might we create a new dietary experience at the Anytown School that will promote the development of lifetime health and fitness?

How might we create a virtual physical education experience at the Anytown School that promotes lifetime fitness?

How might we build a new curriculum at the Anytown School that is based on a design thinking pedagogy and entrepreneurial learning experiences?

How might we use design thinking as a pedagogical approach to engage students in a human-centered approach to learning?

The first three words of the point-of-view statement, "How might we," are important and are intentional. *How* represents that there is a process and pathway for engaging together. *Might* suggests that there are possibilities to explore. And *we* indicates that the experience will be accomplished by designing together. A foundational attribute of the design process is that it is human-centered and deeply rooted in an empathetic understanding of those that you are designing with. The use of *we* in the POV is especially intentional. Engaging those you are designing with as co-designers is a true test of the empathetic intent of design. Design is never done in isolation; it's accomplished collaboratively. As a designer, you never design *for* people; you design *with* them.

DESIGN DRIVERS. My experience suggests that a more detailed vision of the intent of the design is required to really capture the needs of those you are designing with. A set of carefully crafted design drivers, that unpacks the POV, can fully declare the opportunity of the design challenge and provide a complete design framework that will serve as the DNA of the design process.

Depending on the complexity of the design challenge, the design drivers are typically a series of three to six statements that reflect the essential insights that emerged from the evaluation of the information and data collected during discovery. Here is an example of a point-of-view statement and the associated design drivers from a library design project that focused on the transformation of an underutilized space into a space that could support a school district that was consolidating an elementary and middle school building into a single school space.

> How might we recreate a traditional elementary library space to support the development of a preK-through-grade-eight teaching and learning community, post pandemic?
>
> **COMMUNITY:** How might we use this space to create a new heart for the school and a centering location to the school that is welcoming, inclusive, and fun?
>
> **DIVERSITY:** How might we create learning zones in the space that offer a range of learning opportunities that lead to choice, engagement, and student ownership of the learning experience?
>
> **CATALYST AND CONNECTOR:** How might we create a space capable of generating the unlikely collisions and juxtapositions of people and practice that can give rise to new opportunities for teaching and learning?
>
> **LITERACY:** How might we use a new space to support the development of traditional literacy skills as well as the new learning experiences that will extend and amplify what it means to be literate?

MOVING FORWARD. The challenge of the discover and define phases is making sense of a large amount of information obtained during the process, establishing a point of view, and getting the design drivers right. To accomplish this, I present the point of view and design drivers to the stakeholders and ask if they are an accurate representation of the essential elements of the design opportunity. If so, we proceed forward. If not, there is a period of reengagement and revision to ensure that the point of view and design drivers represent the most effective framework for developing potential solutions.

Ideate

In the ideate phase, the goal is to develop as many ideas as possible by using the POV and design drivers as a catalyst for creative thought.

The design process shifts from being convergent to a process that is divergent and generative. Think of ideas as the raw material for the development of a potential solution or solutions. With that in mind, it's important to develop as many ideas as possible. At this point, designers want to encourage quantity. It's important to value all ideas, no matter what the perceived potential of each idea is. In my design projects, I'm always amazed to see an idea that I didn't think would have much relevance become the key to unlocking the creation of the right solution. It's important to understand that all ideas can have their moment. To support this, framing idea statements by beginning with "What if" reinforces that these ideas represent possibilities.

Prototype

In the prototype phase, designers shape the ideas from the ideate phase into a simple representation of a solution. A prototype can be a description of a process, sketches, drawings, renderings, a set of sticky notes, simple physical structures—really anything that can communicate to stakeholders what the solution could potentially be. A prototype is not a finished product but only something that represents a plausible solution. It is acceptable to improve the prototype over multiple iterations until an acceptable version that is ready for formal testing with stake-holders has been created.

Test

In the next phase, the prototype is tested with stakeholders. The time, effort, and kind of testing associated with this phase differs from project to project, but enough time should be spent exploring the prototype to get robust feedback.

Feedback from the testing phase is used in an iterative cycle of improvement that is intended to shape the prototype into an imple-mentable solution. This means that designers can return to any of the phases of the design process to get the additional insights or ideas required to improve the prototype. For instance, testing might indicate that additional information is required from stakeholders, so a return to the discover phase might be warranted. Or feedback could reveal sug-gestions for improving the prototype that might require a return to the ideate phase to generate more ideas for inclusion in another version of the prototype.

What criteria is used to evaluate the prototype? If we've used the design drivers as the foundation for creating a solution, then it makes sense to use them as a lens to evaluate the solution. Iterative testing continues until the prototype is improved to the point where it becomes a viable solution that can be implemented to address the initial design challenge.

Implement

Students are completely capable of designing solutions that matter. Help them to use design thinking to make a difference *now* by putting their solutions into play.

I've included an implement phase in my model because I believe it is important that solutions should translate into action and impact. It's nice to engage students in a process, but that experience must extend into the creation of some product that is applied to the scope and context of the original design provocation and implemented as a solution.

Designers create tangible things as the result of engaging in the design thinking process. Some educators will argue that process is more important than product and that it's enough for students to engage only in the process. But process and product are not mutually exclusive; they are inherently linked. No one stands in line overnight at the Apple Store for the process, they want the next iPhone. The end game in design is to create a solution that matters for humans and implement it so that there can be a real impact.

LOOKING AHEAD

Here's my challenge for readers of this book: How can the six-step progression of design thinking serve as a foundation for a new type of pedagogy? What would adopting a pedagogy like that mean for you and for the experience you offer students? What skills and dispositions would students develop as a result of engaging in design thinking? What would the daily classroom experience be? How can an understanding of design thinking empower you to embrace a new role as an educator-designer?

As you can see, my challenge is a series of provocations that can be addressed through a design thinking approach. As we progress together through this book, I'll return to these questions to help you to uncover your perspectives.

I've given you a brief overview of the design thinking process. To give you an idea of how the process is used, let's apply it to a design challenge in education.

APPLYING DESIGN THINKING

There are opportunities to rethink everything about education and what school is and can be. My introduction to design thinking was through an experience intended to help reimagine the role that the library played in schools. Similarly, I want to provide you with an example of how the design thinking process can be used to rethink a part of the school experience everyone reading this book will be familiar with—the physical education class.

The Challenge: Reimagining Physical Education Class

We've all experienced physical education class. The traditional expectation is that it takes place during third hour with Mr. Jones in a gymnasium where you'll play pickleball (or basketball, softball, gymnastics, floor hockey, etc.) with fifty other students. That has been the PE experience for decades. There is a good reason for this: physical education class gives kids the ability to be active, try different sports, learn team skills, and expend energy—all worthwhile components of a school day.

The COVID pandemic of 2020 disrupted all of this, along with the traditional school experience. Overnight, schools shifted to become online spaces for conducting remote learning. Students became isolated from their peers and schools and had to learn how to learn virtually from home. The challenge to physical education teachers, like other teachers, was to create a beneficial learning experience where participation occurred from a variety of home environments, however those were defined. But the challenge for physical education teachers was different, since their students' experience seemed to require physically engaging in a variety of activities together in the same space at the same time. Planning for a new type of class, where students lacked equipment, every home condition was different, and kids had unequal access to outdoor spaces, became a formidable challenge.

The real impact of the pandemic on the education of students most likely won't be known for years, if ever. It's safe to say that the remote learning experience was less effective than desired. However, there are some emergent trends relating to the physical fitness of students during this time that have become apparent. As a result of the pandemic experience, some physical education teachers reported that students experienced an interruption in skill development, decreased strength and conditioning, and impaired social interaction skills.[1]

But the other realization from the pandemic that has emerged is that remote learning was successful for some students. In fact, there are a growing number of parents requesting that a virtual experience be an option for students moving forward. The pandemic has made it clear that virtual school is a possibility, and that it can work. As a result, it is likely that the number of schools and school districts offering virtual school options will only increase. These options could include virtual physical education courses.

If a traditional physical education class is based on games and teams and grounded by physical activity that occurs at school, what does that mean for a virtual course?

Applying Design Thinking to the Virtual Physical Education Experience

The design process begins by framing the design process with a provocation. In the case of virtual PE, the design challenge could focus on developing an authentic and personalized physical education experience that leverages the unique affordances of modern technology.

DISCOVER. After the provocation has been framed, we are ready to enter the discover phase. We begin by identifying the stakeholders who can offer perspectives associated with the design provocation.

---

1 Kelly Field, "How PE Teachers Are Tackling 'Physical Learning Loss,'" Hechinger Report, November 8, 2021, hechingerreport.org/how-pe-teachers-are-tackling-physical-learning-loss.

Here, I would start with teachers, administrators, students, parents, and the school's technology team. I would then expand my pool to others who could provide insights beyond the immediate experience of school: fitness experts, trainers, and community parks and recreation staff. This is also a good way to make the process more community inclusive.

In my projects, I like to consult artists, writers, entrepreneurs, construction workers, and other professionals from the community to "spike the punch." My goal is to interact with interesting people, understand their perspectives, and use their ideas to inform the design thinking process. Casting a wider net during discovery results in more diverse and interesting perspectives about the design challenge and yields robust and interesting insights.

Once the stakeholders have been identified, I would select a set of ethnography tools as the basis of my discovery approach. For this design opportunity, I would use surveys, interviews with focus groups, charettes with a cross-section of stakeholders, and observations of current physical education classes, if possible.

In my school design work, I use tours of spaces to understand a project's spatial dynamics and a building's characteristics. I ask for different tours: one each from administrators, teachers, and students. By doing so, I can observe each group's focus and perspective about what is important to them. If school is in session, tours conducted during the discover phase help me get an overall view of how the school functions and the experience it offers.

During discovery, it is also important to obtain and analyze preexisting information about the school or district. Web sites can provide interesting insights into what is important and valued. I'd look for mission and vision statements, Portrait of a Graduate documentation, and curriculum and course sequence information to help me understand expectations for the school experience.

DEFINE. After interacting with the stakeholders, I would begin processing the information that I'd collected with the goal of composing a POV statement and a set of design drivers. I'd be looking for the trends and patterns that arise from the interactions with the stakeholder groups.

After analyzing the data, I might develop this POV:

How might we create a virtual physical education experience that supports lifetime fitness and is supportive of each student's unique needs?

In addition to the POV, my discovery approach would enable me to develop a set of design drivers that provide a robust framework for ideation:

How might we create a virtual physical education experience that supports lifetime fitness and is supportive of each student's unique needs? This experience should:

- *be personalized and support student choice in defining their experience,*
- *seek community expertise to inform the design of student learning experiences,*
- *include opportunities for students to interact and learn together as a community,*
- *employ a range of widely available technologies—including those owned by students—to process and document physical fitness activities and personal fitness growth,*

- *be interdisciplinary and integrate other academic disciplines to help students understand and share their learning.*

Before progressing to the ideate phase, I would reengage the stakeholder groups—most likely a representative subset of the original stakeholder group—and ask for feedback. I would use this feedback to refine and improve either the POV or design drivers. When both are in final form, I'd move to the ideate phase.

IDEATE. In the ideate phase, I would develop as many ideas as possible that relate to the design challenge as defined by the POV and design drivers. I like to begin my ideas with "What if" to indicate that this phase is generative and based in developing possibilities.

What if we created a process that helped students develop personal physical fitness goals that would contribute to lifetime fitness?

What if we developed partnerships with local health fitness clubs to leverage their expertise?

What if we could pair physical education teachers with students and local fitness professionals?

What if we worked with the parks and recreation department to develop physical fitness capacities and spaces in their parks? What would this look like?

What if the physical education experience could occur at any time of the day?

What if students used smart watches and cell phones to capture and monitor their physical fitness activities?

What if we developed new assessment metrics for the virtual experience? How would they be defined?

What if virtual-reality experiences were used to support physical education? What if students used virtual reality to exercise in remote locations like Machu Picchu or Iceland?

What if we included science and language arts educators in professional development for physical education educators to help them with designing and supporting interdisciplinary virtual online physical education experiences?

What if we created a virtual education summit for students to share their experiences? What if there were regular online checkpoints for students with their instructor? What would a virtual education online community look like and what would it offer? How could social media support this community?

> I'm going to encourage you to start using the language of "What if." In my opinion, the first step in doing new things is accepting that all ideas can lead somewhere and the use of two simple words can get the ball rolling. Using "What if" is part of the language of the educator-designer.

At this point in the process, every idea is a good idea and should be curated by being recorded. Ideas open new pathways for thinking, new questions for exploration, and interesting directions for the design of a prototype experience.

PROTOTYPE. In this phase, we'll use the ideas from the ideate phase to create an initial prototype. In some of my projects, especially for classroom design, I might create several prototypes. For simplicity, we'll focus on developing a single prototype here. Typically, a prototype is a combination of ideas rather than a single idea.

Here is a plausible prototype experience that uses the POV and design drivers as a foundation and applies selected ideas from the ideate phase. It's likely that in a real process, the first iteration of a prototype would be much different from what you'd end up with. Discussions and improvements with the design team (excluding the stakeholders) would lead to a detailed and applicable final prototype like the following.

> To address the design provocation, the prototype will be a virtual physical education experience composed of fifty students who will work with physical education teachers to define their own physical fitness plan. Teachers (physical education, science, and English/ELA) will undergo professional development with the assistance of local fitness experts and others to define potential options for a student experience that supports student choice and the use of multiple disciplines to understand and represent their progression and growth through the prototype experience. The teachers will also develop a set of evaluative metrics that will be tested during the prototype. Students will have the option to use a variety of technologies (smart watches, VR headsets, blogging tools, and a community portal) to support their virtual experience. These tools will be tested by the school's technology team for wider adoption beyond the prototype experience. The school will provide these technologies should a student not have access. The prototype program will run for one year.

TEST. In this phase of design thinking, the prototype solution would be tested with students and teachers in a live school setting. In my role, I would conduct interviews as the prototype continued over the year and perform surveys of all individuals to assess live progress. I would use the metrics developed by the teachers in the prototype phase to evaluate the overall success of the virtual physical education experience. It is likely that testing of the first prototype would uncover insights that could be used to develop a refined series of prototypes for additional testing.

This iterative process would continue until a solution was developed that was ready for implementation.

IMPLEMENT. Once testing has been completed and a viable solution has been reached through iterative improvement, then it's time for adoption at a larger scale. The goal is not only to develop a solution, but to make it a part of the actual school experience. We don't want to record our process and solution and put it in a binder on a shelf in some administrator's office. We want to implement it so that the solution contributes to a new educational experience.

THE OPPORTUNITY AHEAD

We'll return to the design thinking process throughout the book to continue building your understanding, especially as it relates to a new role as an educator-designer.

To be honest, it took me some time to become comfortable with understanding and applying the process to my practice. There are many moving parts and a new terminology to master. But part of becoming a designer is to adopt a beginner's mindset, try things, and get better at them. That is exactly what I did, and I encourage you to do the same. It's part of the iterative process of learning design thinking.

Design thinking can be used to create and improve any component of a school experience, from envisioning a new course to rethinking classroom spaces and even coming up with ways for how the school day might be redefined. And while all those things are significant, it is truly compelling to think of how the design thinking process could be a foundation for a new pedagogy and classroom experience. It will be interesting to consider how a design thinking approach could advance the educational experience you offer. That's where we are headed. That will most likely be a different approach for you and will require evaluating your current practice. I want to challenge you to consider what you are preparing students for, how you are preparing them, and how you are preparing yourself for a new journey.

CHAPTER 2

Advancing the Educational Experience

Classrooms. The Principal's Office. Gym class. Courses. Units. Lessons. Tests. Grades. A–F. Detentions and phone calls home to parents. Friday-night football games. Great victories and heartbreaking losses. The junior high school dance and all of its drama. Straight, uncomfortable rows of desks. A teacher in the front of the room. The moment the bell rings and your kids don't notice and just keep working because they are so engaged. The same bell ringing for the last time before summer vacation. High school graduation and saying goodbye.

If you've been an educator long enough, you'll probably recognize the moments I described above. Undoubtedly, you could add to my list. And while those I described above are important, even somewhat romantic, what's beyond them? What are the moments that will serve to frame the new school experience and lead students into new conditions as a learner and as a person? How will your classroom experience grow and evolve to provide students with the knowledge, skills, and dispositions that will be required to negotiate a world in constant beta? So, I have to ask a fundamental question: What are you really preparing students for?

There is no question that we are at a unique moment in the history of education. There has never been more opportunity for the profession to address improving the daily school experience of students. At the same time, no time has offered greater challenges to the realization of that opportunity.

It is essential for people—as workers, learners, and citizens—to possess the knowledge, skills, and dispositions to understand, negotiate, and *successfully leverage* the shifting landscape of today's world. It is my belief that schools and teachers must dramatically rethink the daily experience they offer students to help them develop these abilities. It is my belief that a learning experience based around design thinking is part of the way to do that.

In Chapter 1, I provided you with an introduction to design thinking and an example of how it could be used to create a new vision for a physical education experience. And I challenged you to begin thinking about how the sequence of the design thinking process can contribute to the development of a new and robust pedagogy that could support a dynamic and compelling student learning experience. In this chapter, I'm going to ask you to consider three provocations that will challenge you to think deeply about your current practice. This reflection will help you renew your thinking about what is important to you as an educator, what type of experience you provide, and what type you want to provide. I also want to introduce the concepts of improvement and innovation as means for growing and advancing the educational experience that you provide by using design thinking.

WHAT ARE YOU PREPARING STUDENTS FOR?

When I taught biology, I would have said that my goal was to promote the development of scientifically literate students. I wanted my students to be able to pick up a Sunday newspaper and understand the science in the articles they'd find there. Later in my career, when I taught environmental science, I wanted students to understand and appreciate the natural world and find their place in it. I think I was successful at both.

Today, I believe those would still be my goals. For me, they are timeless. However, I wonder if my past practices would still be appropriate for achieving those goals. It's unlikely. Today, the methodologies and resources available for achieving those goals are more robust and would probably contribute to a more effective practice. Further, I would be much more interested in how my students learn and what that would mean, rather than how I taught.

What are you preparing students for? It's a worthy question. How would you answer that question? What knowledge, skills, and dispositions must students have as they move on from school? What about your classroom experience makes it worthy of assembling daily? What type of experience do students want to spend time with, challenges them, provides purpose for them, and is enjoyable to them? What should they experience—not just as students, but as human beings—that will enable them to participate with and contribute to each other, their communities, and to the world?

Perhaps your school has defined these things in some way. Perhaps a vision of this is represented by a Portrait of a Graduate. Perhaps your school's mission and vision statement contribute to an understanding of what is important for students to experience. But if your school doesn't have those things and you have not clearly defined them for yourself, wouldn't it make a great design challenge? Imagine using the design thinking process to answer that question!

HOW ARE YOU PREPARING STUDENTS?

As a teacher, administrator, technologist, digital designer, strategist for an international design firm, and now a freelance entrepreneur and educational designer, I have had the opportunity to see education through a variety of lenses. I also have had the chance to spend quite a bit of time in schools—ranging from public schools and independent schools in the United States to schools across the world, including New Zealand,

Singapore, Mexico, Canada, Costa Rica, the Dominican Republic, and China as well as higher education institutions. To be honest, I still see a lot of what I would classify as traditional practice. And while that's not necessarily a bad thing, I'm left wondering if the current experiences of school will be sufficient for successfully preparing students for their future.

Neil Postman wrote, "Children enter school as question marks and leave as periods."[1] These haunting words reminds us of the childlike wonder that students enter school with and how over time, it wanes, and students become less curious and more compliant. Traditional expectations of what school is, what it offers, and what a student experiences daily works for many kids. But you must wonder if the experience of school truly supports where they can go and perhaps where they need to go. Could there be something not only different but better? More engaging and more effective? More meaningful, more joyful, and more equitable? Could there be a school experience that is based on wonder and curiosity, that leads students on an expedition of the world as well as themselves? Could learning be more than a transactional process between the teacher and student that encourages and recognizes achievement only with a set of simple letter grades? Is it possible to shift to a learning process that is exploratory, engaging, negotiable, creative? Where the classroom experience is grounded by choices made by the learner?

I believe it is possible. It is possible to reimagine the classroom experience. It is possible to reimagine what we have always done as teachers. And I believe that the process of design thinking can help you create this type of experience for your students.

And I wonder how a different experience would prepare students for a life not yet realized and perhaps not yet even imagined. I wonder how the experience of school, and your classroom, could serve to launch their lives.

---

1 Neil Postman, "The American Experiment," *Education Week*, September 6, 1995, https://www.edweek.org/education/opinion-the-american-experiment/1995/09.

Perhaps you wonder the same things. If creating an experience like that is intriguing, and worthy of exploration, how can you and your students get there? To do so starts with accepting that it will be necessary to grow in new directions as an educator.

HOW ARE YOU PREPARING YOURSELF? GROWING AS AN EDUCATOR

I remember thinking that I would really have something once I had spent three years teaching. I just knew I'd have it down. I'd have my teaching materials and enough classroom experience to launch my career and become a great teacher. In fact, I didn't feel comfortable until after my fifth year in the classroom. After building that foundation, I spent my time developing new materials and techniques that helped me improve my craft.

> "The only way to effect real change is to show people a future more exciting than their past, and inspire them to work together on the journey."
>
> **—Bruce Mau[2]**

I think my experience is like that of most teachers. Perhaps it's like yours. Teachers spend time understanding what works with kids and what doesn't. They try things, discard some, adapt others, and incorporate those things that work as useful and important components of a practice. Successful teachers do this, and in my opinion, successful schools are built by teachers who practice in this way.

I want to inspire you to continue improving what you do with students as well as design new approaches, including those that support a design-based pedagogy. I'll be asking you to try design thinking with

---

2 Bruce Mau and Jon Ward, *Mau MC24: Bruce Mau's 24 Principles for Designing Massive Change in Your Life and Work* (London: Phaidon Press Limited, 2020).

your students and see how it works, and how you can employ it in your specific teaching assignment. I'll ask you to assume a beginner's mind-set, with the intent of getting better at using design thinking through iterative improvement. And in later chapters, I'll provide you with the methodology, tools, and resources that will help you use design thinking creatively and effectively.

My goal is to help you build the skills and habits of a designer over time and to inspire you to build on your current practice to create a new teaching and learning experience for you and your students.

ADVANCING THE EDUCATIONAL EXPERIENCE YOU PROVIDE

When I go into a school to conduct discovery, I am intensely focused on understanding who the people there are. I focus on the climate and culture. I arrive in the morning to watch the students arrive and stay to watch them leave. I do classroom walks, where I spend five minutes in a classroom to get a snapshot of what's occurring with teaching and learning. I also spend time with their school report card, their website, their curriculum, and any other documentation that helps me understand the school. I want to understand as much as I can.

My work generally focuses on creating contemporary learning spaces for schools. But it can also mean helping clients develop curriculum and instructional programs, improving their use of technology, or addressing professional growth needs. Regardless of the purpose, I'm there to help advance the educational experience they provide. And in all cases, this will require schools and teachers to grow their practice through a variety of methodologies.

I've heard that people are not necessarily scared of change so much as they're scared of losing something important to them because of a change. So, I'm not going to ask you to throw out the things you've developed that work with kids to help them to learn. That doesn't make sense. And you wouldn't do it anyway. But I am going to show you how design thinking can help you build a classroom learning experience that will be inspiring for students, place them in unique learning situations, and prepare them with the skills and habits that will serve a lifetime. To help you accomplish this, I want to focus on two pathways for creating a design-based teaching and learning experience: improvement and innovation.

Improvement is getting better at something you are already doing. Generally, improvement occurs through incremental and small changes that make something that already exists more effective. Improvement enables a system—a classroom, in this case—to reach a new level of performance by making things that currently exist better. If improvement is not sufficient to meet needs, then we can focus on innovation to create elements for the classroom experience that currently do not exist.

One definition of *innovation* is "the execution of ideas (big and small) that are novel, unique, or haven't been tried before."[3] Another is "the act or process of building on existing research, knowledge, and practice through the introduction or application of new ideas, devices, or methods to solve problems or create opportunities where none existed before."[4]

I mentioned earlier that when I began teaching biology, I realized quickly that presenting concepts visually was a very effective instructional technique. In 1986, that meant taking photographs of images from college textbooks and having them made into slides. By today's standards, it was a primitive process, and it was laborious—by any standard. When I received my first laser disc (think a CD as big as a record album) years later, my capability to employ visual media in my lessons improved dramatically. The new technology gave me immediate access

---

3 Sarabeth Berk, "The 'What's Innovative?' Debate: Try Using First, Best, and Only," Design Gym, April 26, 2021, thedesigngym.com/whats-innovative-debate-try-using-first-best/.

4 Bryan Setser and Holy Morris, "Building a Culture of Innovation in Higher Education: Design & Practice for Leaders," Educause, April 16, 2015, library.educause.edu/resources/2015/4/building-a-culture-of-innovation-in-higher-education-design-practice-for-leaders.

to a whole catalog of both still imagery and video. It improved what I did by providing me with immediate access to a wider range of material. Having the disc also enabled me to create new inquiry-based lessons that blended stills and videos together. The addition of the technology added the capability to create entirely new lessons and be more innovative in how I used media to teach.

I think improvement is straightforward. Innovation is contextual. What is innovative for one teacher might not be for the next. In any case, I think that every teacher has the capacity to improve as well as create and add new things to their practice. Doing both will help you advance the educational experience that you offer. As you gain experience with design, the process will help you to create an environment where both are possible and ongoing, and where you can dramatically shift your practice and how you prepare your students.

STORIES OF IMPROVEMENT, INNOVATION, AND DESIGN THINKING

It is my hope that you experience that one moment that becomes a catalyst for embracing the design process. The most important thing is to take the leap, get started, and grow your capability over time. With that in mind, I want to share two stories with you from educators that will provide perspective on this process and on improvement and innovation. I'd like to begin by introducing you to an educator I deeply respect, Garreth Heidt.

Garreth Heidt, Humanities Educator, Perkiomen Valley High School, Collegeville, Pennsylvania

Imagine giving every one of your students a toothbrush and asking them to discover everything they can about its design. That's exactly what Garreth Heidt does with his students. Heidt believes that studying a commonplace item like a toothbrush teaches students to become critical and creative observers who are curious about how things are designed.

Heidt's approach to the classroom experience is grounded by two questions he asks students to explore: First, why are things the way they are? And second, how can we make them better? These questions frame the design thinking experience of the courses he teaches and provide the foundation for the development of the learning culture he is seeking to build.

Heidt began his career as a middle school teacher. Upon moving to the high school in his district, he was asked to do something different with an English course. He chose to create a humanities course based in design thinking. Years later, he still teaches that class as well as NOVA Lab, a design thinking–based lab experience where students pursue guided and student-defined design challenges.

Garreth freely admits that he has had no formal training in design thinking. But as a learner, he has read widely, taken courses on teaching creativity, and recognized that what he wanted to accomplish in his classroom was embodied by a design thinking approach. Initially, he struggled with this approach because he was always being pulled "back to the safety of teacher while the beautiful, dangerous, and ultimately more interesting possibilities available in what was fascinating me about design was pulling me forward." To progress, he kept at it, took steps forward and backward, and continually assessed his development.

Ultimately, he realized that the adoption of design would require fundamental shifts in how he practiced his craft. This required him to improve planning and project management and get better at messaging to get kids to buy in when they knew that "design was his thing." Beyond improvement, he had to develop new systems for allowing students to have more freedom while still holding them accountable. He also realized that his physical classroom setup was not suitable for design activities, so he had to create a new spatial identity that could support a design experience.

Over time, Garreth has been able to create a classroom experience in which students have time to explore real questions and even linger to promote their curiosity about the world. He believes that a shift to design thinking has helped students become more intellectually engaged and develop a creative mind that makes connections, creates solutions, and is prepared to meet the world and "do great things."

Glenn Robbins, Superintendent, Brigantine Public Schools, Brigantine, New Jersey

Like Heidt, Glenn Robbins recognizes that teachers are greatly influenced by the traditional expectations of what school is and how a teacher should practice their craft. He says that teachers have always been told what they must do to meet those expectations. But in his role as superintendent, he sends a different message. It is his goal to create a culture where teachers are empowered to take risks, to explore, and to "cross the threshold" into a new and different type of classroom experience. He wants teachers to know they can do things differently.

During his time as teacher, principal, and eventually superintendent, Robbins has been a proponent of applying design thinking to the classroom experience. He recognizes that the most significant impact of the adoption of this process is giving up control and giving agency to students to have ownership of their learning experience. This means that teachers must adopt a different role; Robbins sees teachers as a catalyst for the learning experience. He suggests letting the kids drive everything. Robbins suggests walking into the new experience like you don't know anything and being totally open as a learner. Consume everything you can about design thinking—books, YouTube videos, everything.

To adopt a design thinking pedagogy, Robbins believes that teachers must possess a growth mindset and maintain a positive attitude. He believes that success is dependent on being open, enthusiastic, and comfortable with taking risks. He also adds that it is important to not try and do it alone. He advises that you should partner with another teacher or group to provide support and to push you forward.

Most importantly, he has seen that a design thinking approach opens opportunities and enables students to have a wider view of what school can be and how they can be involved. For example, students in a school he has led have used design to create solutions for a local hospital to make it more child friendly. In his current school district, students became designers to imagine the transformation of a dated library into the new community hub of their school. Robbins has seen this kind of engagement make even the most disinterested students come alive and get energized about school.

The single biggest outcome of a shift to a design thinking approach? Robbins says that it is increased student participation and ownership of their education.

LOOKING AHEAD

I began this chapter by listing a set of moments that are typical of a traditional school experience. They are good things, and they will most likely characterize school for a long time. But a school experience doesn't have to be limited to those moments; it can be more. It's time to contribute new moments that will build on and advance the school experience.

> To help you reflect on the three questions I posed in this chapter, I've created a design exercise. It's available on the book's website for you to use. This reflection will help you quantify your current beliefs and the status of your practice. This will give you a starting point to work from and to eventually gauge your progress and impact as you create and implement a new classroom experience.
>
> **davidjakesdesigns.com/educatordesigner**

There is no doubt that there are challenges associated with this. The two educator examples I just presented make it clear that addressing and overcoming the traditional expectations of the role of the teacher in the school experience is a critical step. Teachers must also address their own perspectives about their role and practice. As I mentioned previously, adopting a design thinking pedagogy does not mean that you must discard your previous practice, but it can help you build upon the successful elements of your pedagogy so that you can advance the classroom experience you provide. This will require that you challenge yourself to consider what you are preparing students for and how you are doing that. It will also require that you reflect on how you are preparing yourself. It will require an open mind and a willingness to return to become a beginner and learner again. It will require taking risks, experiencing failure and success, undergoing course correction, and believing that new moments can be created for the school and classroom experience.

In the upcoming chapters of this book, I will introduce the techniques and strategies that will lead to a set of innovative approaches that will support a design thinking approach to teaching and learning. I'll also help you understand and make sense of the shifts that are required to develop a new perspective about the role of the teacher in the educational experience. My goal is to help advance your practice and promote the development of a new mindset and new role: the educator-designer.

CHAPTER 3

A New Role for the Classroom Teacher:
The Educator-Designer

When I began my new position at an architectural firm, I entered a culture that was very different from what I'd experienced in education. There was a new language, new ways of working, new types of spaces, the responsibility of winning new clients, and an expectation that my skills and experience would give the firm a competitive advantage. And there was the dreaded requirement of the weekly timesheet, where your time working on projects had to be documented down to six-minute intervals. I worked on Michigan Avenue in Chicago in a corporate design studio of sixty thousand square feet with 250 designers creating solutions for education and the healthcare industry. To say that this environment was different from my school experience would be an understatement. But after I got my footing, I was able to use my abilities as a learner to adapt and grow into my new role.

The most significant outcome of my experience was developing the ability to see the world through design. That's a lofty statement, but it's true. Through a daily exposure to design, and through a deep immersion in the process, I developed a different way of thinking, perceiving, and acting. I developed a different mindset, a different lens, and new ways to focus on thoughtful and creative actions and outcomes. That took some time—and to be honest, the process continues today.

As an educator, how you *think, perceive, and act* form the basis of your professional practice. As you proceed through this book, I'll challenge you to develop a new mindset (how you think), develop an additional lens (how you perceive), and understand how to direct your lens to develop a focus (what the lens is attentive to, what you act upon) for your work. A new mindset, lens, and focus will help you to grow past the traditional expectations of teacher and school and contribute to the ability to assume a new role as an educator-designer.

In Chapter 2, I encouraged you to evaluate your classroom practice through the exploration of three essential provocations. The goal of that activity was to help you establish a snapshot of your current reality that can serve as a baseline for understanding your growth and improvement. In this chapter, I'd like to present a plausible future for any educator willing to make the leap toward a new classroom experience by using design thinking. If this future resonates with you, it can provide a vision of a practice to work toward developing. Comparing this future against your current reality can identify the gaps between now and a future state as an educator-designer. Any gaps that are present will help you understand where you need to improve current practice and where you need to be innovative and create new components to your practice.

That can be intimidating, but it's also truly exciting.

THE EDUCATOR-DESIGNER BELIEVES THAT LEARNING IS BOUNDLESS

Opportunities to learn are everywhere. What happens to the classroom learning experience when it extends past the traditional boundaries of the four walls of the classroom and the physical constraints of the school? What happens when the opportunities to learn extend past the homogenous conditions of the typical classroom environment into more authentic and diverse community locations? The educator-designer sees their community as a source of boundless learning opportunities.

There is no situation that is more "real" than school, but learning confined within the footprint of a school building is not as authentic as it could and should be. When I taught ecology, I took my students on a four-day field trip to northern Wisconsin, where we studied ecological concepts in streams, forests, and wetlands. You can't understand the use of plants by indigenous cultures until you pick a sprig of wintergreen and chew it to uncover how it tastes. You can't understand forest succession until you see thirty-year-old three-inch-tall sugar maple trees just waiting for their chance at sunlight. And you can't understand stream ecology until you get in one, turn over the rocks, and see the diverse assemblage of aquatic insects that form the basis of its food chain. There was no better way for students to learn the principles of ecology than to immerse them in the diverse conditions for learning that the experience afforded. I often thought that students learned more in those four days than they did at any other time in the school year. Exposure to diverse conditions for learning promotes the wonder and curiosity that is necessary for understanding the natural world and the people and things that inhabit it. It is inspirational and can connect students to their responsibility for creating and shaping their world.

In my opinion, the deepest type of learning occurs when students are placed in unexpected and unfamiliar moments when they must activate and rely upon the learning skills and dispositions they possess. When these moments engage students with people that are different from them, they can promote the sensitivity and understanding required to negotiate the similarities and differences that exist among people. To accomplish these outcomes, the educator-designer embraces an expanded vision of learning that enlarges the boundaries as well as the vision of the educational experience.

Almost every mission statement from almost every school includes the words "lifelong learning." As educators, we all want our students to learn over the course of their life. What that means, exactly, is open for interpretation, as is the process required to acquire the knowledge, skills, and dispositions of someone who can actively seek to learn across the span of their life. To help you think of this in a different way I want to introduce you to a model of learning that has greatly influenced how I think about the potential of a new school experience. It's a model that expands the traditional perspective of lifelong learning to include two additional domains: life-wide learning and life-deep learning.[1] This model can enlarge your mindset, shift your lens, and deepen your focus on a more thoughtful and dynamic kind of learning that design thinking can support.

Lifelong learning is learning that occurs across the timeline of a person's life—it's linear. *Life-wide* learning broadens the concept of learning to include the knowledge and understanding acquired *through life experiences* at any point along that timeline. For example, knowing how to negotiate a new airport, what to do when injured or sick, what to do when you lose a wallet, or how to effectively give a child advice are all the result of experiential learning that most likely occurs beyond the school experience. It's learning that occurs as the result of a variety of life experiences. By broadening (widening) the experience of students at any point along their lifelong trajectory, schools can enrich their learning experience and their lives.

Life-deep learning focuses on developing the qualities of being human, such as having the ability to show empathy and compassion toward others; persistence, honesty, and truthfulness; providing service to others; and how to act and behave as a member of society. Life-deep learning develops because of the meaning and richness of the experiences that a person has over a lifetime. These serve to help develop the qualities of the human self.

---

1 James A. Banks et al., *Learning in and out of School in Diverse Environments*, LIFE Center, 2007, http://life-slc.org/docs/Banks_etal-LIFE-Diversity-Report.pdf.

The educator-designer believes it is possible to make school-based learning more experiential and that these experiences contribute to life-wide learning. It follows that more experiences, and the right experiences, will foster life-deep learning.

The addition of life-wide and life-deep learning to lifelong learning creates a three-dimensional model of learning (length, breadth, and depth) that provides a rich and comprehensive scaffold for the development of learning experiences by the educator-designer. How we connect these three dimensions to the growth and development of children represents the good stuff—and it's what makes the future of education so exciting.

The more varied experiences that you have in life, the greater opportunity you have to develop the qualities of being human. And the more experiences students have—especially those that are rooted in a human-centered design approach based in empathy—the more the likelihood that they will develop the knowledge, skills, and dispositions that contribute to a life worth living.

THE EDUCATOR-DESIGNER USES A DESIGN THINKING–BASED PEDAGOGY

Pedagogy refers to the theory and practice of learning.[2] It represents the interactions between the educator and student that serve the learning process.[3] Additionally, I see pedagogy as the instructional approaches that are used not only to teach curriculum content but to also help students develop the skills and dispositions of learners. The pedagogy of the educator-designer is based on the six-step design thinking process but can include other instructional methodologies that you already know work.

---

2 "Digital Pedagogy: A Guide for Librarians, Faculty, and Students," University of Toronto Library, August 25, 2021, guides.library.utoronto.ca/c.php?g=448614&p=3061959.

3 "What Is Pedagogy? How Does It Influence Our Practice?," Child Australia, accessed January 14, 2022, childaustralia.org.au/wp-content/uploads/2017/02/CA-Statement-Pedagogy.pdf.

What could a design-based pedagogy look like? What would happen if you posed a design provocation to your students; they engaged stakeholders to understand them, their identity, and their needs; and then your students used that information to develop a point of view and design drivers that formed the framework for the design? What if they then went through an ideation process, prototyped a potential solution, tested it with their stakeholders, and then improved the design to the point where it became an acceptable solution that was implemented? Your students would have just done design.

Imagine teaching a whole course where the curriculum included a series of questions (not content-based units) that required students to employ design to solve real problems for real people, right now.

And think of the opportunities for exploration, inquiry, collaboration, interdisciplinary connections, and the use of technology. Think of the opportunities for deep intellectual engagement, the development of empathy, productive struggle on the part of students (and the teacher!), creativity, and the development of the skills and dispositions that will help students negotiate an unpredictable future. Think of the opportunities to engage students in real work that matters. Think of developing the skills and dispositions that promote lifelong, life-wide, and life-deep learning.

A design thinking pedagogy creates empowering relationships between the learner and their world. Imagine a learning experience that presents students with the opportunity to engage through multiple ways of thinking, knowing, creating, and acting. Imagine a learning process where the outcome is not just individual growth and development as a learner and person, but an experience where students contribute their ideas to create solutions that make an impact and make their community a better place.

Keith Nuthall, principal and cofounder of Odyssey STEM Academy in Paramount, California, says, "High school doesn't have to be practice. It can be the real thing."[4] I couldn't agree more.

THE EDUCATOR-DESIGNER CREATES LEARNING ENVIRONMENTS THAT SUPPORT A DESIGN THINKING—BASED EDUCATION

There is no doubt that the spaces of a typical school limit the type of experiences that occur within them. Most of the classrooms I encounter are inflexible, uncomfortable, and limited in their capacity for supporting a diverse pedagogical approach. In my project work, teachers have revealed to me that they don't spend a great deal of time considering space when they develop lessons. That's easy to understand; the space as it is can't contribute much to the lesson.

As a designer who specializes in creating contemporary learning spaces, I have seen my share of school spaces. Many of the classrooms I see are dated and obviously designed for the traditional teacher-centered learning experience: rows of older desks, with a teacher desk or station at the front of the room, whiteboards, and some type of technology display—sometimes interactive. That's still the standard in most schools today.

So it's time to rethink the relationship between space and teaching and learning. That begins with a renewed willingness to explore what classroom spaces can be. It requires understanding how the school's community, and the locations within it, constitute viable learning spaces. Most importantly, the educator-designer must recognize the role of space in learning and actively seek to create learning environments that support students cognitively, socially, and emotionally.

---

4   Keith Nuthall and Becky Perez, "Odyssey STEM Academy: A Conversation with Keith Nuthall and Becky Perez," Education Reimagined, June 17, 2020, https://education-reimagined.org/odyssey-stem-academy-a-conversation-with-keith-nuthall-and-becky-perez/.

Making a shift to a design thinking pedagogy requires more from a typical classroom space. This is true of physical spaces such as classrooms, but it also applies to virtual spaces that are used today as part of the school experience. Virtual spaces are here to stay, and moving forward, more capable and connected online spaces will be essential for supporting a new type of hybrid learning experience.

There are other challenges associated with creating new conditions for school learning spaces. Rethinking and improving physical spaces is expensive. Creating virtual environments that are engaging and uniquely leverage the capacity of technology to add value to the learning experience is another challenge. But both are interesting design provocations for any educator-designer.

THE EDUCATOR-DESIGNER SHAPES THEIR PRACTICE USING DESIGN THINKING

As a classroom teacher, I was evaluated several times a year. An administrator visited my classroom, recorded a narrative, and then conducted a post-evaluation meeting with me to discuss their perceptions of my lesson and ability to teach. Usually, I knew they were coming and prepared accordingly. At other times, they just popped into my classroom to say hello and see what I was doing.

Sometimes those events were helpful, but mostly they were of little value in helping me improve my practice as an educator. I'm certain that my colleagues felt the same way. These visits were just part of what we had to do. I'm not sure I ever looked at them as an effective measure of my ability or a way in which I could obtain feedback that would help me become better at my craft.

Advancing the educational experience that you offer and taking the steps required to assume a new role as an educator-designer is predicated on having a methodology that will empower you to independently understand your practice as well as create a pathway for continual evaluation and purposeful growth.

Fortunately, there is a process that can help you do this.

It's the design thinking process.

What if you used discovery as part of a self-evaluation process? As you know, the first part of the design process entails understanding everything you can know about the people you are designing for. In the case of your classroom experience, that means focusing on understanding your students. But it also means focusing on understanding yourself and your practice. Engaging in an ongoing and reflective discovery process helps you understand your students as people as well as their academic progress, your actions and behaviors as an educator, and the overall effectiveness of your practice.

There should be a continual flow of information that informs efforts to improve and to innovate. An ongoing evaluation of the classroom experience will provide you with information to help you understand what you need to improve and what you need to create.

Additionally, design thinking provides a methodology for internalizing the evaluation of your practice and how it impacts students. Using the process in this way will help you to assume ownership of your growth as an educator.

I have developed a set of ethnography tools that you can use to conduct discovery about the effectiveness of the experience you provide. They can be downloaded from the book's website for your use.

davidjakesdesigns.com/educatordesigner

THE EDUCATOR-DESIGNER PROVIDES AN EQUITABLE LEARNING EXPERIENCE

During discovery events such as a classroom observation, I must remain very aware of how I process what I see and hear. I spent fifteen years as a classroom teacher and twelve as an administrator, so it's important that I not let my educator lens influence my observations. I find that I must remind myself constantly of this when I think about how I would have conducted the lesson if I were in the teacher's place! That is not my job. My job is to objectively observe and be nonjudgmental. I'm trying to capture the experience, not evaluate it. As a designer, my role is to observe, listen, record, and engage in sense-making around the experience.

In my design work, I am constantly challenged to consider how I design workshops, how I ask questions, how I interact with my clients, and even how I dress. To some extent, that's a normal expectation. But I can't approach the design process through my lens as a white male. That's not fair, and it's not an approach that will ultimately yield an equitable design solution. I must engage with a deeper sensitivity and understanding of my own biases to be able to understand my client's needs. But that can only happen when you have become deeply aware of your own "identity, values, emotions, biases, assumptions and situatedness."[5]

I'd like to challenge you, as an emergent educator-designer, to design with an empathetic lens, but also through an equity-based approach that encourages acceptance and inclusion.

I always taught five classes of around thirty kids. That's 150 kids that I had to understand. Each has their own family life and their own background, their own way in which they like to learn, and each has their own level of interest in your course and even in learning. That's

---

5   Tania Anaissie, Victor Cary, David Clifford, Tom Malarkey, and Susie Wise, "Equity-Centered Design Framework," Stanford d.school, accessed January 16, 2022, dschool.stanford.edu/resources/equity-centered-design-framework.

the challenge of teaching thirty different learners with different needs, abilities, and interests.

And I approached that by creating a one-size-fits-all educational experience.

• • •

Creating a different learning experience begins with creating a different classroom culture, where diversity is recognized and celebrated. This requires that individual and cultural differences represented within a classroom population are recognized and factor into the design of the experience. This approach recognizes and values diversity rather than ignoring it in favor of a sterile process designed for educational efficiency. Taking the first step to embrace a new role as an educator-designer requires that you understand yourself and the biases and prejudices that you bring to the classroom. That's a challenge and it takes time, effort, and humility.

When visiting and working with schools around the world, I had to learn to be more careful about the words I used, how I presented myself and greeted people, and even how I designed presentations to ensure that I used culturally appropriate colors and imagery. It's a big task to recognize and understand your own beliefs and abilities. To address them in the context of an equitable design process is a worthy challenge. It's a continual work in progress, and to develop the objective lens required for success as a designer is always an ongoing effort.

The next step is even more challenging; it requires you to use a similar lens to view your students. It's easy to prejudge based on appearance or the way students dress or who their friends are. Perhaps you know that, and I'm stating the obvious. But in a school, educators encounter all types. And it's always important to remember that every student has value, something to contribute, and is interesting in their own way. An educator-designer values multiple perspectives and personalities, embraces new ways of thinking and interacting, and approaches and interacts with people with a sensitivity that leads to an equitable and inclusive classroom experience.

Let's consider how the process, improvement and innovation, and the educator-designer role blend together to create a design thinking classroom.

CHAPTER 4

The Design Thinking Classroom

The first three chapters of this book have focused on developing an understanding of the design process, exploring growth and improvement, and defining a new role for the classroom teacher. In the remaining chapters, I'll address the pragmatic steps that will enable you to realize this role and use design thinking to create new experiences for you and your students.

Embracing the role of an educator-designer will undoubtedly mean shifts in the way in which you practice. It follows that this will cause shifts in what you and your students experience daily in class. To help you understand what this could look like, I want to give you a picture of the essential elements of what I consider to be the core of any educator's practice as they manifest in a design thinking classroom: curriculum content, instruction, assessment, technology, and space. This chapter will also include my thoughts on how students are impacted by these shifts and what you can realistically expect from them.

CURRICULUM CONTENT

Through the content of your course, students get to experience the world. Through the teaching of your curriculum's content, students can develop the knowledge of an educated person.

It's unlikely that you will be able to individually change content standards and what is expected to be taught. That is not the intent of this book or the shifts I am about to describe. Rather, a part of the role of the educator-designer is to find the story in the content and the authentic context for teaching it. Authenticity provides a reason for learning the content. And finding an entry point for a design thinking–based instructional process will be an essential component of a new classroom experience.

What is the real reason you teach what you teach? How do you connect and apply your course content to the world beyond school? Why would students be interested in learning what you teach?

I'm going to recommend that you evaluate your curriculum content through a lens of empathy. Are there entry points in your subject matter where you can develop empathy-based provocations? Find the potential for real, human-centered meaning in your content. Find those points and use the design process to create design thinking experiences for students.

With those entry points, your course can become a series of provocations that create authentic contexts for learning and gives kids a real reason to care and engage. For example, instead of studying cell division and mitosis, what if there was a provocation associated with the challenges associated with being diagnosed with cancer? (More on how that would work in the next chapter.) While the course content can remain relatively static in most cases, it is entirely possible (and recommended) that these provocations change from year to year as events in the community and world provide additional contexts for study and exploration.

INSTRUCTION

It's almost impossible to create a generalization about the instructional environment of all classrooms, but I'll try. In my experience as an educator and designer, I've observed that most classroom experiences are teacher-driven. The teacher plans and conducts the lesson. The pathway for learning is prescribed by the teacher, and students progress through the lessons together, in a predetermined sequence of instruction.

Over the years, much good has occurred in classrooms structured in this way. Teacher-driven instruction, or direct instruction, can be engaging and valuable. And sometimes it's necessary. My junior and senior biology students would not have understood homeostasis unless I lectured and explained it to them. The topic is just too complex.

Direct instruction has its place. But in a design thinking classroom, the learning experience can be so much more. In a design thinking classroom, students engage as members of a collaborative design team that explores a design provocation through discovery and inquiry. Students are active and curious participants who have agency to direct their learning as necessary. The classroom learning space may look different each day as learners design and redesign the space to meet their needs. Technology is used to create prototypes and artifacts and connect student-designers to stakeholders and experts beyond the physical classroom. It's messy, noisy, and active.

> "Don't plan the journey for them, go on the journey with them."
>
> **—Christian Long**[1]

The role of the teacher in this classroom shifts from directing and leading the experience to serving as a guide and mentor who shapes and guides process and progress. The role of the educator—now an educator-designer—shifts from being a content provider to orchestrating and supporting the way students negotiate the design thinking process to address real world questions and issues. The learning experience becomes co-constructed by the students and teacher.[2]

---

1 Christian Long, conversation with the author, September 2016.

2 Maureen Carroll and Laura Mcbain, "Where Empathy Meets Learning: Exploring Design Abilities in K–12 Classrooms," *Voices from the Middle* 29, no. 1 (2021): 14–17.

Throughout the design experience, there are learning goals that focus on mastery of content knowledge as specified by the course curriculum. There is an emphasis on building learner skills and dispositions and those that are necessary to engage in the design process. This type of learning environment, matched with the curriculum, can then provide a reasonable pathway for the development of experiences that support lifelong, life-wide, and life-deep learning.

ASSESSMENT

Making the shift to a design thinking classroom will require rethinking the purpose and processes of assessment. This reevaluation includes a consideration of what gets assessed, how it gets assessed, and the role that students play in the overall assessment process. In the spirit of design, I'm going to recommend that assessment should be ongoing and iterative. It should also provide the feedback required to improve what students know, what they can do, and how they act as learners and as people.

Learning through a design approach is based on authenticity, and the way students are assessed must reflect that. We can't measure the tasks and behaviors of the design thinking process with traditional assessment tools like multiple-choice tests and pop quizzes. The type of assessment must be aligned with the expectations created by the student experience, and the assessment itself must authentically measure the student's ability to engage in design thinking, as well as the products they produce and their overall learning progress.

Like the traditional classroom, it will still be important to measure content knowledge. Evaluating the growth and development of skills and dispositions developed because of engaging in design thinking will be of equal importance. It follows that assessment must include methodologies that ask students to demonstrate content understanding and those that enable students to represent their learning with the artifacts and products associated with design challenges.

I have said before that I'm not asking you to eliminate elements of your practice that you know work, and that's true of assessments, too. Perhaps there are times when a multiple-choice test might be appropriate. But I think it's important to push you to expand your approach on how assessment occurs in your classroom. The design thinking classroom should include some form of portfolio assessment. Look for an opportunity for students to partner with you to co-evaluate the products they produce because of engaging in design, and multiple ways to measure their progress in terms of developing knowledge, skills, and dispositions.

There are practical considerations involved with this, mainly class size and the time required to examine student artifacts. But I would ask you to start small, try this type of assessment on for size, and see how it works. And I would strongly encourage you to put yourself through a design thinking approach and develop a working model of a prototype student assessment program. Work with your students to build and refine a new hybrid assessment program that measures their progress and that is doable for them as well as you.

TECHNOLOGY

There is no doubt that the pandemic of 2020 stimulated robust discussion about remote learning and the value of technology. Regardless of the debate, in the design thinking classroom, technology serves as an invaluable partner to create a broader canvas for design work while providing students with creative and generative capacities.

During my work as an instructional technology coordinator, our learning management system was most active from 11:00 p.m. to 1:00 a.m. While most of the teachers were probably asleep, students were most active on the system. In my opinion, there is value in providing an always-on, always-available, connective platform for teaching and learning that supports the synchronous and asynchronous interactions required for learning.

This perspective is supported by the reality that professional work now views the workplace as a hybrid of synchronous and asynchronous and remote and in-person. Schools should adopt a similar posture with regards to the spaces that are available for teaching and learning. Preparing students to negotiate this physical-virtual world also prepares them to interact with others in both environments, how to network, and how to use technology productively and appropriately. In addition to a learning and work platform, technology provides the tools to conduct design work, to manage information from ethnography, and to create reports and presentations, among other uses—all valuable applications. But the true value in technology is found in its capacity to create communities that connect people across distance and time. Developing these communities so that they add value to the learning experience requires an empathetic understanding of student needs, their access to technology, and the guidance necessary to apply networked technologies to student learning.

SPACE

What if we were to reimagine your classroom as a design studio?

This will require thinking beyond the traditional classroom setup of steel-frame desks arranged in rows with a teacher desk in the front. A design studio needs to support a variety of design-based activities, including collaboration, whiteboarding, prototyping, presentations, and discussion. These activities require a flexible and agile space capable of adapting in the moment to student needs. Optimally, a school design studio should have tables that provide surface area for project work, a variety of storage options for design materials and ongoing projects, portable and wall-mounted whiteboards, ample electrical outlets, and connective technologies.

There is also a need for a capable virtual space that extends the capacities of the physical space. It's important to consider that a virtual space can provide 24-7 access to design resources and a variety of online tools (shared document creation, graphics editors, discussion boards, etc.) useful for engaging in the design process and connecting student-designers with each other and the people they are designing with. A virtual space can also serve as a learning space on its own, independent of the physical space, if necessary. Realizing that capacity requires a more thoughtful, connective, and human approach than what was employed in remote learning during the pandemic.

I would like to recommend that you enable students to decide how they use the studio space for design, transferring ownership of the space to students. Of course, there will be times when you need to have the space arranged in a certain way. But I see many classrooms every year, and one of my observations is that they always reflect the teacher. Creating student-centered spaces that celebrate students and their accomplishments goes a long way to creating spaces that students want to spend time in. This is also a critical step in developing inclusive learning experiences that engender a sense of belonging.

Finally, begin thinking that the spaces of the school's community are locations for learning that offer unique expertise, spatial conditions, and resources that enrich the learning process. In my opinion, expanding the learning experience beyond the formal locations of school is a critical aspect of the future of the school experience.

There is a lot to consider about rethinking the relationship between space and learning. As a classroom teacher, you may not have the ability or agency to make all of the dramatic changes to your classroom space as I have just identified. However, there are steps that you can take to make your space more design friendly. (I'll provide strategies for this in Chapter 7.)

STUDENTS

Most likely, using design to learn will be very different for your students. They know how school works, and they know how to play the game of school.

Being patient with students will be key; a design thinking approach is not how they have done school before. They might be frustrated and anxious, and it's important to recognize this and talk about it. You can expect that it will take some time, effort, and practice to move beyond typical learning behaviors from the past.

Preparing students with the skills required to engage in a full design process will contribute to easing their concerns about new methodologies and approaches. That's good teaching. A great way to start with a design thinking-based approach is to work on simple but specific experiences that build students' design *skills* and their ability to engage in the *process*.

Using design thinking with your students will enable them to develop the knowledge, skills, and dispositions of a designer. If the process is applied as a learning (or instructional) framework as part of a pedagogy, it's easy to see its value. Students learn how to address a complex and ambiguous question and manage uncertainty. They develop a heightened sense of empathy and continually develop their ability to ask questions, listen, and probe for deeper understanding. They learn how to process data and draw conclusions. Beyond those abilities, students develop ideas and explore how to shape them into plausible solutions. Most importantly, they learn that they can create meaningful products and solutions that improve the lives of people that they are designing with.

The process for creating design thinking learning experiences is scalable and will help you take logical steps into the design process, regardless of your current assignment and familiarity with design thinking. The strategies that I will show you in the next chapter will help you to get started with building design skills, deepening student understanding of the design process, and engaging student designers in learning experiences that matter.

CHAPTER 5

Designing the Student Learning Experience

Chapter 3 was about defining the role of the educator-designer. Chapter 4 described the design thinking classroom. In this chapter, I want to describe the techniques and strategies that will connect the educator's new role to a new classroom experience based in design thinking.

DO YOU REMEMBER MITOSIS? TEACHING CELL DIVISION

All high school biology teachers teach their kids about cell division. It's an essential part of understanding how living organisms grow and develop. You may remember the components of the process of how a living cell goes from one to two—interphase, prophase, metaphase, anaphase, and telophase.

In my cell division unit, I had several lessons that taught students about the steps of mitosis. Basically, I lectured about the process while writing notes that were projected on a screen. The students dutifully wrote down the notes in their notebooks, memorized the facts about each phase, took a quiz, and generally did well. A week or so later, after additional lessons on other topics, the students took a multiple-choice test on cell division where they had to remember the facts of cell mitosis again. That test was the culminating event of the unit. On to the next unit!

Three weeks later the kids couldn't remember anything specific about mitosis. If they were to retake that same quiz, most would not have performed as well as they did previously. There could be many reasons for that, but looking back on it many years later, I could have done much better as a teacher in connecting mitosis and cell division to a meaningful reason for learning them in the first place. As a fifteen-year-old studying biology, what meaning did the unit have, other than a chance to successfully pass a test, complete a course, and fulfill a graduation requirement?

The experience of my biology class followed a tried-and-true path. The unit was introduced, we did the lessons of the unit (with quizzes interspersed at appropriate locations), reviewed for the test, took the test, and reviewed the test and the correct answers. Repeat for the next unit. The learning culture was:

> I'm going to tell you about biology.

> You need to learn this before you can learn this.

> What you learn, and how you learn it, is determined by the teacher.

It was predictable and proceeded in a very linear fashion. Admittedly, kids developed an understanding of biology, but I'm not sure they ever *experienced* learning biology and made the necessary connections that biology and science could, and should, have made for them in their lives. My biology course was driven by the curriculum and my interpretation of the curriculum into an orderly progression of direct teaching and passive learning.

There is more to teaching and learning than that. Using design thinking, we can reshape the lesson into an experience, change compliance into active participation, and shift the learning culture of the classroom from the expected and predictable to one based in wonder, curiosity, and discovery.

At the end of this chapter, we'll revisit my unit to see how the design thinking process could be used to rethink how students could learn cell division and how that study could be made as relevant and meaningful as possible. I think the example will serve to stimulate your thinking and help you to visualize how the design thinking process can support a new teaching and learning experience.

At this point, here are questions that I want to pose to provoke your thinking: How might we create learning experiences that are based in wonder and curiosity? If we were to visualize that, what would it look like? What are the methodologies and techniques for creating learning experiences based on a design thinking pedagogy? How might we create open-ended inquiry explorations that follow the design thinking pathway?

RETHINKING THE EDUCATIONAL EXPERIENCE: INTRODUCING THE "SQUIGGLE"

The experience of my biology class could be represented by the following simple model.

A represents the start of the unit; the straight line represents the series of lessons that composed the unit; and **B** is the culminating event, most likely a multiple-choice test. The course syllabus declared a series of A-to-B sequences that, taken together, made up my course.

There is an alternative to this model. It's what I call the "squiggle" (seriously), and it represents what I think a learning experience in a design thinking classroom could look like. Here it is:

Provocation
an invitation into learning

Resolution
...or more learning

Experiences
pathways for discovery and inquirty

This model begins at the left side of the drawing with a provocation that initiates a series of learning experiences for students that are exploratory. Each takes learners in different directions and down the rabbit holes that help them develop the understanding and insights necessary to address the provocation. The nonlinear experiential pathway in the center of the diagram reflects that learning is rarely a linear and sequential series of events. Rather, it's made up of a set of experiences in which students pursue their own questions in search of meaning through discovery and inquiry. During this time, there are opportunities to generate ideas, create initial solutions, experience failure and course correction—all to reach a resolution to the original provocation.

> "Curiosity involves a willingness to engage with complex, unfamiliar, and challenging concepts or endeavors."
>
> **—Todd Cashden**[1]

1 Markham Heid, "Curiosity Is the Secret to a Happy Life," Elemental, February 13, 2020, elemental.medium.com/curiosity-is-the-secret-to-a-happy-life-3dc5d940d602.

Ultimately, the learning journey is shaped by the learning itself, where the learner has multiple paths for the exploration of the provocation. Throughout the learning process, there may be additional questions that emerge and lead learning in different and interesting directions. It is this exploratory process of discovery that reintroduces wonder and curiosity into classroom learning.

The experience culminates when students compose an initial response to the original provocation. Or, better yet, when learners uncover additional questions for future exploration. They can then reengage the squiggle to develop a more complete understanding.

My challenge to you: Could your classroom become a place where students were challenged by a truly authentic provocation, engaged by a series of learning experiences based in inquiry, and used their understanding to craft an original response to a compelling design provocation?

GETTING STARTED

I think it's interesting and aspirational to provide a theoretical model that challenges the boundaries of the traditional educational experience. Doing so pushes and expands the mind and helps people to begin thinking differently.

> "There is nothing more dangerous than standing still in a world that is changing."
>
> **—Jacques Chirac[2]**

But now it's time to take that model and make it something that can inform actual classroom practice. We can translate that model into a pragmatic set of strategies that will help create a design thinking classroom. The strategies are designed so that any educator can use them

---

2 Madelaine Drohen, "Ready or Not, the Euro Is Coming," *Journal of Commerce*, May 1, 1998.

within the context of their current assignment to begin shifting the classroom experience.

Making the shifts necessary to create a design thinking classroom will require a beginner's mindset, a willingness to adopt a try-fail-recover-and-improve perspective, and a persistent belief that design thinking can lead to an engaging and compelling classroom experience. Most immediate shifts may be small. In some cases, shifts might be dramatic. The important thing to do is to make a shift.

And . . . to have the courage to go where the shift takes you.

That means adding unpredictability and uncertainty back into the teaching and learning experience. Using design thinking can reshape linear and predictable classroom lessons into diverse learning experiences that support inquiry and curiosity and—most importantly—have real meaning for students.

EMPLOYING A DESIGN-BASED PEDAGOGY: THREE STRATEGIES

Let's start by exploring three strategies for developing a design thinking classroom. Together, these strategies will help students build design skills, understand how the process works, and apply the process to addressing provocations and challenges that matter.

Strategy One: Build Design Skills

The first step toward success in a design thinking classroom is to help students master the skills that will enable full participation in a design thinking experience. You can help students do this by creating and implementing simple experiences that target *skill development.*

When I taught my first project-based unit on ecology, I used the growing local problem of invasive Canada geese. I thought it would make a great topic. What I learned was that fourteen-year-old high school freshmen weren't that concerned about Canada geese. I became frustrated by their lack of interest, but more importantly, by their lack of the ability to engage in project-based learning. My real mistake was believing that they had the learning skills (questioning, research, collaboration) necessary to be successful in that type of experience. I was wrong. My advice is to build a design thinking classroom by first building students' skills and competencies. Beginning with skill-building experiences will also help you build your confidence as an educator-designer and your ability to use design thinking with your students.

You can use activities that require only twenty to thirty minutes of classroom time, are easy to create and implement, and focus on helping students develop a single design skill. These are learning activities that you can use within your current pedagogical practice, and they will help students to think critically and creatively. Most importantly, they support your transition to a practice based in design thinking. Begin slowly with activities like these and build your repertoire and experience over time.

To create more starter experiences like these, use the chart of student design skills available on the book's website.

davidjakesdesigns.com/educatordesigner

To get you started thinking about what this might look like, here are some possible activities that will help students build design skills.

MAKE OBSERVATIONS. Promote observation skills in students by having students make observations about a set of images or a video. Have them develop and share four or five observations. Be sure to help them understand the difference between an observation and an interpretation or hypothesis.

ASK QUESTIONS. Give students a simple design provocation. Have them develop three questions that they would ask to engage a group of stakeholders in a discovery process that addresses the provocation.

Then, have them identify what they think is their best question and share. Develop a class list of questions. Developing great questions is the first step in creating an impactful solution.

DEVELOP LISTENING SKILLS. Have students listen to an audio recording (or a video without the imagery) and record salient points associated with the recording. Or conduct an interview with several students and have the class listen and record important points.

DEVELOP A POINT OF VIEW. Promote students' ability to develop a point of view. Give them a set of data/observations and ask them to create a point-of-view statement.

CREATE IDEAS. Ask students to develop fifteen ideas about how to improve a simple object, perhaps something in your classroom space. The goal is rapid ideation and helping students stretch their thinking. The activity focuses on developing as many ideas as possible and helping students understand that any idea is a good idea.

DESIGN A PROTOTYPE. Give students a set of ideas and ask them to develop a quick sketch prototype. Or ask students to select a common item in your classroom and develop a prototype that improves the functionality of that item. Be sure to stay within a twenty-minute time frame; the focus should be on action and representing ideas quickly and in a tangible way.

COLLABORATE. Create a twenty-minute experience designed to support the development of collaborative skills and dispositions.

WRITE COLLABORATIVELY. Create an experience that enables students to develop the skills of writing together in an online document. This could be a synchronous event, where writing and editing occurs together in real time, or an asynchronous experience, where students contribute to a document or improve the work of their group members at different points within a certain time frame.

CRITIQUE. Engage students in a discussion of how to provide feedback to others that is reflective, empathetic, and useful.

CAPTURE PICTURES WITH YOUR PHONE. Capturing digital imagery during discover phase events is an essential skill for any designer. Ask a student team (three to four students) to capture images of your class engaged in any design activity to practice capturing important moments in the ethnography process.

LEARN A TECHNOLOGY TOOL. Take twenty to thirty minutes to introduce a technology tool that students will use to support design thinking activities.

To further develop student design skills, consider linking several skill activities together to create a deeper experience. The goal is to target a single skill, such as questioning or ideation. Begin with an activity and extend it with another that is complementary. Here are some examples:

COLLABORATIVE IDEATION. You might expand the twenty-minute ideate session into a full class period by having each student select their five best ideas (out of, perhaps, fifteen) and post them on a wall (using sticky notes). Students then do a gallery walk and extend other students' ideas by adding their own with another sticky note. The goal of the two activities together is to first develop ideas and then crowdsource additional ideas that either improve or add to the original set.

DEVELOP GUIDELINES. Use the twenty-minute critique discussion of how to provide feedback on designs and then ask students to collaboratively develop a set of five guidelines they believe would be most valuable for critiquing student work.

Strategy Two: Build Process Skills

The second step in building a design thinking classroom experience is to help students develop design thinking process skills. These experiences help students to build connections between the different steps of the design thinking process.

These experiences are more complicated and require more classroom time to implement and complete. A good rule of thumb is to allocate 100 to 150 minutes to successfully complete each of these activities, which can be used within the context of your current pedagogy.

IDEATE-PROTOTYPE-TEST-ITERATE. Have students develop their own prototype ethnography tool and provide time for classmates to use their critique guidelines to offer suggestions and insights for improvement. Provide time for students to adjust their tool based on this feedback.

DISCOVER-POINT OF VIEW-DEVELOP DESIGN DRIVERS. Have the class use their ethnography tools, or other tools that are available, to conduct ethnography around a provocation. Have each group use a specific tool and present the results. Then pool the class's data, and have each group develop their point-of-view statements using the combined data. Expand the point-of-view statements into a set of design drivers. Compare and discuss the outcome of the development of the design drivers.

VIRTUAL ETHNOGRAPHY-SYNTHESIS-EMPATHY MAP. Use the above activity but have students convert their ethnography tool into a digital format so that they can use it within a virtual collaboration tool. Have students work with another class or other groups in your class to conduct a virtual ethnography event. Have them synthesize the data they have collected using an empathy map (discussed in the next chapter).

A MINI DESIGN SPRINT: THE TALISMAN. This activity takes place over three full class periods. Have students develop a list of questions that enable them to interview a class member to discover who their interviewee is. Have them use this information to develop a point of view about who their interviewee is by defining three personal attributes (design drivers) that they find interesting. Using those as design drivers, each student then prototypes a talisman (an artifact designed to bring good luck to a person on a journey) using simple found materials. Have them present the talisman to the person they are designing it for to test their design and to also engage others empathetically.

> A list of commonly found materials that can be used in proto-typing activities can be found on the book website.
>
> **davidjakesdesigns.com/educatordesigner**

Strategy Three: Build the Designer

A goal of shifting to a design thinking classroom is to promote the development of student-designers. To accomplish this, students must have the opportunity to use the entire design thinking process to address design challenges. This requires rethinking the traditional unit-based curriculum and engaging students through a provocation-based design thinking approach.

This is what we have been working toward with the previous two strategies. It focuses on creating an experience that enables students to use and demonstrate the design and process skills that they have developed.

In a perfect education world, an entire course would be built around a series of design and process skill challenges with students eventually growing into the ability to engage in a series of design challenges where they learned curriculum content, built the skills and dispositions of learners and designers, and actively addressed issues by developing and implementing solutions.

MY EXAMPLE: REVISITING MY CELL DIVISION UNIT

Let's consider my original cell-division unit and apply these three strategies to rethink the unit as a range of experiences.

Build Design Skills

In the context of building design skills, I might start by focusing on developing my students' ability to ask questions. I could use a thirty-minute experience that asks students to generate questions about cellular division and what they would have to know to understand the process. This experience could introduce mitosis in my traditional cellular division unit.

Additionally, having students work in collaborative groups could help them develop collaboration skills. I could extend this experience to as much as sixty minutes by asking groups to identify their two most important questions, share them, and develop a class list of questions for exploration.

Build Process Skills

The centerpiece of my traditional cell-division unit was the two-day mitosis lecture.

The replacement activity would begin with a provocation: "How does a cell go from one to two?" That would start a three-hour (or three-classroom-period) experience. For this experience, I wouldn't ask them to engage in the discover or define phase of design thinking; instead, I'd ask them to collaborate and draw from their knowledge of cells (an earlier unit of instruction). I'd provide them with online media sources of cell division (video, still frame imagery) that do not include sound or text—only visual information—that they could access from their laptops. Giving them access to a variety of multimedia raw information that they must interpret encourages the development of visual literacy and design skills: observation, interpretation, and sense-making.

I'd then expect them to process the online media and use their understanding of cells to develop ideas (ideation) about how the process happens. My expectation would be that they use these ideas to develop a plan (the prototype) for how cell division happens by assembling their ideas into a cohesive strategy that addresses the provocation.

To work on additional skills, I could have them present their plans, which the other groups would evaluate (perhaps using the critique guidelines developed earlier). Based on feedback, each group could then modify their original plan (testing and iterative improvement).

Most likely, there would be some time for me to clarify and clear up any misconceptions or holes in their thinking.

In this experience, students would work on ideation, prototyping, collaboration, and developing visual literacy skills. If we extended the experience further, they might also be required to present, listen to feedback, and modify their original model.

I like this sequence much better than my two-period lecture. The drawback is that it will take more time. However, the experience is much richer, students will have a chance to develop a range of process skills in addition to content knowledge, and my role shifts from being a content provider to becoming a conductor of the experience.

I should mention that in these examples I am still using the traditional approach of a content-focused instructional unit. But—and this is critical—I have begun to use strategies and experiences to begin transitioning my practice to a complete design thinking approach.

This is almost the entire design process, but it misses the most essential part: designing using a human-centered approach that sees the challenge through an empathetic lens.

What would that look like in the context of my cellular division unit?

Build the Designer

Using a pedagogy based in design thinking, I could replace my entire cell-division unit with a complete design experience. I typically spent between fourteen and seventeen class periods on this unit. I believe I could spend the same time—or perhaps slightly longer—on a more powerful and beneficial experience.

A provocation that links cancer to the cell-division process provides the authentic context for a design process. (A note of caution: Students may have parents, siblings, a relative, or a friend with cancer. It's important to consider this—but engaging students in real issues in the right way helps them grow as learners and as empathetic people. That's just my take.) Generally, cells divide, and then they stop. Sometimes this goes haywire, when the genetic control of the cell-division process fails to operate properly. Cells can then keep replicating out of control—a damaged cell creates more damaged cells. These form masses called tumors, which may inhibit organs and other body functions—and possibly cause cancer.[3]

To launch the experience, I would ask my student designers to address the challenge of supporting children that have been diagnosed with cancer.

To start, students would have to engage with a variety of groups to develop an empathetic stance on the provocation (discover phase) and acquire the insights needed to develop a point of view. This could be teachers, doctors, cancer support organizations, or even cancer survivors.

Using this information, students would develop their insights and perspectives into a point of view and design drivers. I would expect that each collaborative group might interpret information differently and develop similar but different drivers.

---

3 "Cell Division and Cancer," ABPI, accessed February 1, 2022, abpischools.org.uk/topics/cell-division-and-cancer/cell-division-and-cancer/.

Once these drivers had been established, students would enter an ideation process where they'd develop ideas around how best to support children with cancer based on the design drivers. These ideas would then be assembled into a prototype solution (like a product or program) that would be tested with the same focus groups from the empathy phase (and perhaps others) with the goal of improving the prototype.

The student assessment for this challenge would be designed around the completion of the steps of the design process as well as evaluating elements of the final design solution.

The next step would involve actual implementation of the solutions. Students can design meaningful things that help their fellow human beings! Why not start when they are in school? A great example is the students from Design Tech High in Redwood City, California, who have created a prototype of an early cancer detection system.

↻ **Design Tech HS Retweeted**
Elena Avesani @elena_avesani · Oct 24, 2018 ···
@dTechHS students showcasing their prototype of early cancer detection solution at #OOW2018 @ORCLCitizenship #OracleVolunteers #techforgood #proudoraclecoach #designthinking

It's still important that the students have a chance to achieve content goals. When and where necessary, you could build in a lecture or other traditional methodology into this process. Adopting a design-based pedagogy doesn't mean that you give up everything that you have learned is successful.

ANOTHER EXAMPLE: HEALTHY DIETS FOR KIDS

Helping students to understand and develop lifelong fitness should be a goal of any school. All students in K–12 schools engage in lessons or participate in courses that focus on this goal. A curriculum could be composed of interesting and applicable design challenges that form the basis of an experience where students engage in the design thinking process to understand their own health and fitness.

Let's form a design challenge around making healthy choices for lunch using a sequence that includes activities that develop design skills, develop process skills, and develop the designer. The first two stages of this sequence could support a traditional pedagogical approach or be used to support a full design thinking experience, as described in the build-the-designer step.

The design provocation could focus on improving the school lunch experience so that it contributes to a healthy lifestyle. This design challenge is broad enough that students could explore many directions. Perhaps it is about personal decisions that the student needs to make. Perhaps the cafeteria's options limit the opportunity to make effective, healthy choices. Perhaps there is a lack of understanding of what constitutes a healthy diet. Perhaps some condition at home gets in the way. There is a potential for student groups to develop very different point-of-view statements that lead to very different design directions and solutions.

Start with Skill-building

Students could work in collaborative groups to develop an ethnographic tool to be used with stakeholders in the empathy phase. For example, one group of students could develop questions for a survey. I would also have my students interview other students at different times and locations during the school day to work on questioning and data-recording skills.

Focus on Developing Process Skills

To build process skills, students could conduct ethnography activities using the tool they designed. Each group collects data and then presents it to the class, contributing to a class-wide data set. This set of design activities focuses on creating and implementing ethnography tools, conducting discovery, and assembling and presenting information.

Build the Designer

Each group could then use the class data to develop design drivers. Following this, student groups would use ideation and prototyping to develop a product/resource for healthy eating that could be tested and improved. Each group then presents their solution to the class and a panel of school and community members. Depending on the outcome of the presentations, a set of solutions could be implemented to improve the student lunch experience.

In this chapter, I focused on three strategies that can be used as a framework to create experiences that support design thinking. I believe it is important to start small and build on your progress. Begin by developing student skills while building your confidence in the design thinking process. I think that this is the logical way to introduce new classroom design experiences. From there, focus on building the process skills that can lead to students engaging in the entire design process. Perhaps that is a semester capstone design experience that leverages the design and process skills that your students have developed. With time and with experience, your classroom can become a place where students use design thinking to engage real questions and create solutions for people that matter.

CHAPTER 6

Classroom Tools for Design Experiences

As a classroom teacher, I used a traditional set of tools to determine if my students understood what I was teaching. Tests, quizzes, worksheets, and homework were the typical instruments I used to gauge understanding. I also relied on qualitative insights to understand my kids: the questions they had, their body language, and just the look of the entire class. After a while, you can just tell when they don't understand something.

Looking back, my assessment tools were standard and probably presented a limited picture of my students' performance and how they were learning.

As a designer, I employ a very different approach when I work with clients. The ethnography tools and techniques I use to see into the lives of the people I am designing with are intended to be comprehensive and inclusive. My intent is to obtain the information and insights that are required to develop solutions that matter. I learned many of these tools and techniques at the design firm I worked at, and since then, I've prototyped and refined more of my own. These have been created to get the right information from the right stakeholders at the right moment.

The goal of this chapter is to introduce you to the ethnography tools and techniques that are used during the design process. The strategies and tools that are discussed in this chapter represent standardized ethnography tools. Not all tools are used in every design challenge. Over time, I would encourage you and your students to develop your own tools that support your classroom design thinking experience as you become more experienced with the process.

As an educator-designer you can use these tools and techniques in three ways:

1. To better understand your students so you can design more effective learning and classroom experiences.
2. To empower yourself to improve aspects of your professional practice.
3. As part of a design pedagogy, to help students address a provocation and develop solutions.

To jump-start your use of design thinking, digital files of the ethnography tools that I mention in this chapter, as well as others, are available for you to download. These are published with a Creative Commons CC BY-NC License and can be downloaded and freely used for noncommercial purposes by teachers and students with suitable attribution.

davidjakesdesigns.com/educatordesigner

GETTING STARTED

Identifying Stakeholder Groups

As planning for discovery begins, it is essential to identify stakeholders. Who are the people who will be influenced by the outcome of the design process and need to have input when designing for a solution? These are your stakeholders.

When identifying the individuals and groups that should be engaged in the discovery process, designers focus on developing a representative and inclusive assemblage of people. As you might expect, there are limits to who can be engaged. Designers can't talk with everyone. They can't visit every site. Over time, and with experience, you will build an understanding of the right mix and number of individuals and groups that should be included as participants in discovery activities.

If you are using design thinking to understand the needs of your students, then your stakeholders are your students and possibly their parents. If you are seeking to improve your practice, your stakeholders might be students, other teachers, parents, and administrators.

If your students are using design thinking to explore a design question, the list of stakeholders depends upon the design challenge. A generalized list might include various school and community groups. For example, in the student-health design challenge from the previous chapter, a list of plausible stakeholders might include other students, teachers, administrators, parents, cafeteria workers, and food service managers. It can be important to include other individuals and groups that can offer insights beyond the immediate stakeholders. Students could also engage dietitians, athletic and fitness trainers, scientists, and others who offer a range of expertise. In other design challenges, professionals such as artists, musicians, poets, and futurists might be added into the mix to provide unique and creative perspectives.

What's most important is that by engaging people in the process, they become part of the process. It's been my experience that when you involve people in developing directions and solutions, there is a greater chance that the outcome of the process will be impactful. Being inclusive and bringing people into the process is an essential aspect of a human-centered approach to design.

General Ethnography Tools Used During Discovery

After the stakeholder groups have been identified, a plan for discovery can be developed that identifies the ethnography events and tools that will be used to engage them. Most of the tools are intended to be used face to face, but they can also be used as part of a virtual engagement.

Here are the basic ethnography tools that I like to use during the discovery and empathy phase.

SURVEYS. I generally begin my engagements with a survey that helps me understand who I am designing with and to inform other discovery events. Good surveys are a challenge to write, so be sure to test and prototype any that you or your students create. Asking students to develop (write and prototype) a survey is a great opportunity to promote critical thinking, questioning, and design thinking skills.

Remember that it's impossible to meet with everyone in person. Using a survey can be a great way to be inclusive and offer participation to a large group of community participants.

WRITING PROMPTS: Prompts should be simple to create, generative, and used to get people engaged immediately.

I like to use prompts for stories that are limited to six words or that can be printed on a postcard (or note card). For example, I might have stakeholders write a six-word story on the future of learning. Or I might use a completion strategy, asking respondents at the end of a design engagement to fill in the blanks: "I used to think _____, now I think _____." For students, I might ask them to complete a sentence beginning "I learn best when _____." These usually provide interesting insights that can be explored in a discussion.

OBSERVATIONS: Simply watching and observing how things work and how people interact is an essential component of ethnography. Everything can be important and tell you something. For example, I spend time observing students arriving at school to begin the day, the cleanliness of the school, passing periods, and anything that can provide me with an opportunity to see the real and everyday engagements of the school. I spend time in classrooms doing full fifty-to-sixty-minute classroom observations. I also do a classroom snapshot walk, where in two hours, I spend five to ten minutes in as many classrooms as I can.

TOURS. Tours are an essential component of understanding how things work together. For example, if a design challenge involved creating signage for a community park, a tour would be essential for understanding the context of the design.

In my own design work, I ask people to take me on tours of their physical location and explain how things fit together and function. This has helped me learn things I wouldn't have otherwise found out. For example, on a tour of a high school, I once saw a track hurdle in a long hallway. This caused me to ask specific questions about athletic practice facilities with administrators and coaches, and I learned that the track team needed to use the hallways for their practice.

Always ask to be taken to a space that is never on any other tour. I have ended up in some unique places that way, including a middle school crawlspace!

In a school-design project, I'll ask to take three tours of a school: one led by an administrator, one led by students, and one by teachers. I end up getting three different tours and three different perspectives.

INTERVIEWS. Interviews are a staple of ethnography work.

Start by defining who will be interviewed (these are called focus groups) and then prepare discussion questions. Many times, these questions are created from the survey responses you want to know more about or find interesting. Don't be afraid to go down rabbit holes with follow-up questions to participant responses. That's where the really good information is. But most importantly, spend your time listening! Interviews are not a time for presenting information; they are intended to engage stakeholders and enable them to help you understand the landscape of the design challenge.

I always record interviews to transcribe later; if you want to do so, always ask for permission.

CONDUCTING DESIGN CHARETTES

Charettes are design workshops conducted in groups of between fifteen and thirty individuals that can last anywhere from an hour to a full day or more. The workshop is generally composed of groups of four to five individuals working as a design team with a set of ethnography tools. Each team should present their work for each tool and then be ready to answer questions. The discussion that follows is very helpful and insightful.

Here is the basic strategy: Create charette groups, explain the purpose of the day to the participants, and initiate the engagement by having them write (using, for example, a six-word-story prompt). Then select two or three charette-specific ethnography tools, depending on time and need. Have the groups engage by writing or sketching ideas on sticky notes and placing them on each tool. After each round, each group should present their outcome. Then repeat the process with the other tools. Be sure to photograph the participants engaging in the process and all data to create a record of the event.

Charette-Specific Ethnography Tools

These tools are designed cognitive frameworks that stimulate charette participants' thinking and provide a way to organize their ideas and insights.

It is possible to take any of these tools and place them into a digital whiteboarding tool that will enable participants to provide answers and feedback in a virtual charette. This will enable you or your students to engage groups in discovery activities that might not be local to your school.

I've found the following examples to be successful in engaging stakeholders and drawing out their perspectives, but it is important that you and your students begin to develop your own tools that work for your engagements. Use these examples as models and modify them. Start by adding your own headings and axes to the two- and three-column tools and the two-by-two grid.

Find a list of more ethnography tools on this book's website.

davidjakesdesigns.com/educatordesigner

TWO-COLUMN TOOLS. Divide a 24" ×36" sheet into two columns, and use each column to explore one of two potential outcomes. Here are some examples of two-column tools that I use in my charettes. What column headings could you use to develop your own two-column tool?

TAKE FORWARD / LEAVE BEHIND. What would you take forward into a new learning experience from your current experience and what would you leave behind?

IT'S NOT ____ / IT'S ____ . This format can show how the ongoing process of the charette influences and shifts thinking. This can be completed in real-time during the workshop.

TOO MUCH OF ____ / NOT ENOUGH OF ____. Ask stakeholders what they do too much of and what they do not do enough of—in class, or elsewhere.

TEMPLATE   **TOOL**

Too much of...	Not enough of...

THREE-COLUMN TOOLS. Divide a 24" × 36" sheet of paper into thirds to explore three potential outcomes of a question.

> **FIRST/BEST/ONLY.** "When were you the first, best, or only at something?" I often lead off with this tool, which always creates a great discussion and gets charette participants to think deeply. It's a good way to measure the innovation capacity of an organization.[1]
>
> **TELESCOPE/BINOCULARS/MICROSCOPE.** Use this tool when you want your groups to consider the impact of something or evaluate something from different perspectives and user distances. In my practice, I often ask stakeholders to consider an issue from a school district, school, and classroom perspective. Alternatively, I can shift the scale to ask about impacts to school, classroom, and student.
>
> **START/STOP/CONTINUE.** Use this to understand what participants want to start doing, stop doing, or continue doing.
>
> **WHAT WORKED / WHAT DIDN'T WORK / SUGGESTIONS.** Use this to evaluate a process, technique, or event.
>
> **ANTIQUATED/CLASSICAL/INNOVATIVE.** Ask: What is an old, outdated practice? What is something that you know works? And what practice represents fresh thinking and action?

---

1 Sarabeth Berk, "The 'What's Innovative?' Debate: Try Using First, Best, and Only," Design Gym, https://www.thedesigngym.com/whats-innovative-debate-try-using-first-best/.

TEMPLATE

TOOL

				Antiquated	Classical	Innovative

YOU / CONSTRAINTS / COULD BE YOU. Use when you want to iden-tify the current conditions of something (You) and what a future preferred state might look like (Could Be You). Between these two headings sits the Constraints section, where participants provide responses regarding the roadblocks that prevent them moving from You to Could Be You.

TWO-BY-TWO GRID. Create a grid with four cells when you want to inquire about four potential outcomes of a question. Here are two examples.

ERIC (ELIMINATE, REDUCE, IMPROVE, CREATE) GRID. Ask participants what they would eliminate, reduce, improve, or create about something they currently experience or have experienced. For example, you could use this with students to understand their overall school experience or to evaluate your course.

TEMPLATE   **TOOL**

Reduce	Create
Eliminate	Improve

IMPLEMENTATION GRID. Use this when developing potential solutions to understand their potential impacts measured against the difficulty of implementing them. Participants place solutions (on sticky notes) in the appropriate quadrant to assess their viability (measured by considering the potential impact vs. the ease/difficulty of implementing that solution).

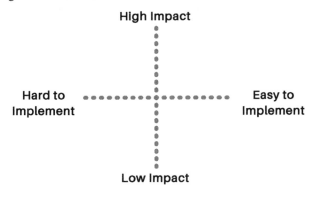

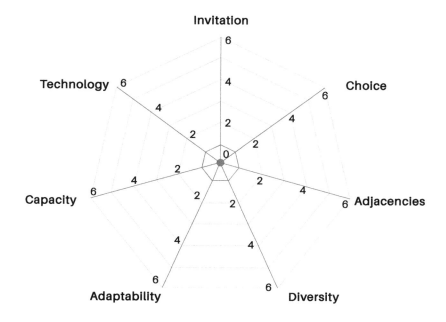

RADAR CHART. Radar charts are useful when you want to evaluate multiple factors that relate to a question. You can have each participant connect their dots and fill in the space to create a visual map of their data, or have each participant complete their own chart and then plot their answers on a group radar chart to see the whole group's responses.

I've used this radar chart with stakeholders to have them evaluate how their classroom space functions considering seven factors. A value of 0 means it does not support that quality, a value of 6 is a maximum value associated with support.

VISUAL LISTENING. At some point, people run out of ways to describe something. Having them interpret visual images that are strategically chosen to represent some component of the design question is one of my favorite techniques. You can also lay thirty to forty images on tables and have participants take a gallery walk and use sticky dots to vote on an aspect of a design question. Use six each of red (dislike), green (love), and yellow (mixed feelings) dots to indicate preferences, and a single blue dot to reflect a favorite, most important image. Follow this up with a discussion to understand the trends that emerge.

EMPATHY MAP. This is a tool used by designers to help them process what they've perceived during a charette. Individual designers self-reflect about an engagement with a group using the tool, and then they assemble as group to share their insights.

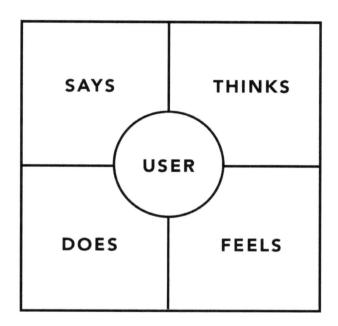

Charette Supplies

Design charettes do not require an extensive list of supplies. Keep it simple. Here is what should have on hand in your design studio:

ETHNOGRAPHY TOOLS. For a charette, I print these tools out on 24" × 36" paper (you could also use 18" × 24") to use with participants organized into design teams. Each team gets one. The tools can be created easily in a presentation tool like PowerPoint or Keynote and exported as a PDF. I print them at a local print shop that has a large format printer.

STICKY NOTES (VARIOUS COLORS): Use sticky notes for people to write their ideas on. I have found that participants like to move their ideas around, and using sticky notes to record answers facilitates that. Use colors strategically to categorize response types.

BLACK MARKERS. Use markers (such as Sharpies) to encourage people to write in big block letters, which enables other charette participants to see ideas when they are presented or during a gallery walk. Use black because you'll want to photograph the notes. Avoid ballpoint pens, which are hard to see during presentations and difficult to photograph at a distance.

STICKY DOTS (VARIOUS COLORS). These are useful for voting on ideas or indicating a preference for an idea or response.

BLANK TYPING PAPER. Use this to make name tents and for other general uses.

CAMERA. Use a camera to record the events of discovery and to take pictures of the data from a charette. A cell phone camera is usually sufficient, but you can use a DSLR if there is a need for higher quality photography that might be used in promotional materials or in reports. Always ask for permission before engaging in any type of photography.

Seeking Patterns and Trends in the Data

In the discover phase, designers generally collect a lot of data. Collecting it and managing are two challenges. The third challenge—and the whole point of discovery—is making sense of all of it.

Full disclosure: I'm not a statistician (B's in college). I don't expect you or your students to be, either.

Here are some basic strategies for analyzing your data.

HAVE CHARETTE PARTICIPANTS HELP YOU. After the use of a particular ethnography tool, and before discussion, have participants use two or three sticky dots to indicate what they think their most import-ant ideas are. For example, in a three-column tool, they could identify their two most important ideas per column. This is also helpful for them when they present their insights as it focuses their presentation.

USE AN EMPATHY MAP. Design teams should use an empathy map as soon as possible after a design charette to capture and organize their insights. When I travel home from an engagement on a plane, I typically use the time in the air to write seventy-five statements about what I learned. I can normally get to fifty or so quickly. Interestingly, I usually struggle with the remaining twenty-five. I have found that this intellec-tual process really helps me to get past the obvious stuff and reach into what matters.

USE QUESTIONS TO INTERROGATE THE DATA. What patterns and trends are obvious? What do we need to know more about? What rabbit holes can we go down? What is the most important thing we know now that we didn't know before? Generate a list of common questions that you can ask about data.

TAKE QUALITATIVE TRENDS AND CREATE QUANTITATIVE DATA. Follow up on insights gained from discover phase events by creating surveys that enable you to generate quantitative data. For example, a general trend from a charette might be that participants think that classrooms should be more agile; using a survey to ask about that might indicate that 72 percent of the respondents felt this way.

MAKE YOUR DATA AND INFORMATION VISIBLE. Use software to create visualizations of data that can serve to illuminate patterns and trends in the data.

In the next chapter, we'll address the design of learning environments (physical and virtual) that support teaching and learning through a design approach.

CHAPTER 7

Creating Learning Environments That Support Design Experiences

I've mentioned my first classroom, a typical school space with rows of tables for two, a teacher station, and a blackboard. That was it. Oh, and some storage. Throughout my teaching career, I taught in different iterations of that space. It was always the same, except for the addition of a computer and the change from blackboards to whiteboards.

Looking back, I can honestly say that I paid little attention to space and its impact on how I taught and how my students learned. My spaces couldn't do much, so I didn't really consider the role that space could play when planning lessons. When I reflect on this now, I realize that all the spaces I taught in had very little capacity to support a diverse range of teaching and learning experiences.

Today, in my role as a space designer, my goal is to change that. The challenge? I still see the same rows, with the same steel-frame desks (chair and desk connected as one) that were designed over a century ago in classrooms. Imagine that—students are still sitting in furniture that was designed well over a century ago. I also see quite a few desks that were purchased in the 1970s, along with fifty-dollar sterile, uncomfortable chairs that have been retrofitted with tennis balls on the legs to prevent them from making awful sounds when they are moved on the classroom's tile floor. A large teacher desk (and sometimes two) is always present in the space, equipped with a computer that is usually tethered to a digital projector on the ceiling. Posters, anchor charts, artifacts, and other materials that take up valuable wall space complete the picture.

And in my travels, with all the different types of spaces I visit, see, and use, I've found that schools are the only spaces like this. The world has long moved past any similar type of design, but in schools, here we are. Still.

It's safe to say that most school spaces limit the learning experiences that students can have. For example, if the space is difficult to rearrange, the teacher is less likely to engage in collaborative learning opportunities. That's easy to understand, and it's no fault of the teacher. Sometimes it's just too hard. In some cases, it's impossible. Can those spaces support a design-based learning experience? Fortunately, the answer is yes—with modification.

In this chapter, I'll be discussing the characteristics and development of teaching and learning environments—both physical and virtual—that can support a design thinking classroom experience. This will begin with a discussion of physical spaces and then address the creation and use of successful virtual environments. And I'll give you practical recommendations and strategies that can empower you to shift your classroom to a next-generation learning environment capable of supporting a design thinking experience.

THE VALUE AND MEANING OF THE WORD *CLASSROOM*

Before we go too far with rethinking things, let's remember that the traditional classroom has served education, teachers, and students for decades. Much good has taken place in that space. But the classroom that I still see in most schools was designed for a different era and for a different expectation of what school prepared students for. Today's world demands that students possess new skills and dispositions. A redesign of the typical classroom can create an environment where this is possible while still honoring the timeless tradition of the student-teacher relationship.

The classroom is still the predominant location of learning in schools, and it's unlikely that will change anytime soon. It's still the location where students who want to learn meet the adults who will help them do that. We can't lose that. But we can reimagine the spaces of school to make them more capable of supporting new experiences that prepare students for their futures.

THE ECOLOGY OF LEARNING SPACES

It's important to design spaces so that they work together. How spaces connect and form a network—an *ecology*—of interdependent spaces that amplify each other's purpose and capacity is a compelling design question. How could classrooms, library, cafeteria, and corridor spaces be designed to work together, each with its own uniqueness and affordances, to provide an interesting array of spaces that support a continuum of learning opportunities? Together, an ecology of spaces designed in this manner provide more capacity than any single space considered on its own.

It's essential to consider the role that virtual spaces play in this ecology. Imagine how the combination of virtual and physical spaces, along with virtual-reality experiences, could create a truly dynamic learning environment! Imagine how virtual spaces could expand where teaching and learning occurs and how student-designers interact with stakeholders and experts beyond their school.

No single space can offer everything for students and teachers. Creating a range of spaces from physical to virtual provides a spectrum of choice for students that can drive new learning opportunities. Creating a design thinking learning experience will require that learning occurs across a range of spaces, from physical to virtual. What could that look like?

CHARACTERISTICS OF LEARNING SPACES

I'm going to suggest a basic model for the creation of a design studio that can provide a starting point for thinking about how physical and virtual spaces can work together.

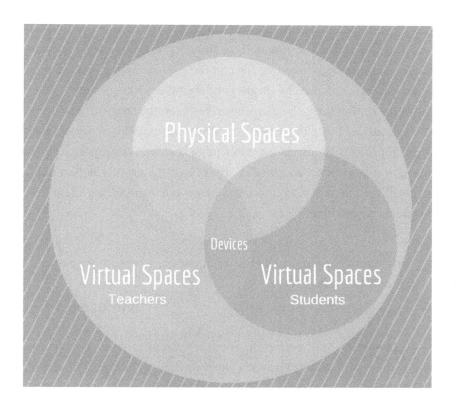

The model is anchored by physical spaces, which would include your current classroom space. Connected to this space are two virtual spaces, each characterized by different degrees of ownership. There is a virtual space assigned to teachers, which might include access to a learning management system (LMS), a digital grade book, or other online tools that the teacher has control over. There is a virtual space for students that might be composed of tools that are used principally by them for their class design work. Tools that students use but are not part of a school's technology platform could also be considered as part of their space.

It is likely that there would be shared ownership and use of both virtual spaces. Students would spend time in the teacher's virtual space (for example accessing documents from the LMS) and vice versa (teachers accessing and making comments on a student group's online document).

It is important to note that the conduit for interacting in all of these environments is formed by a variety of digital devices (phones, tablets, and laptops) that form the connection between the spaces.

The model I just presented is a shell, one possible representation of a comprehensive learning environment that would support a design thinking experience. As a model, it represents a prototype that could be modified, altered, and improved based on information uncovered through a design challenge.

> "Classroom spaces should tell us about our students, who they are, and what they value."
>
> **—Thomas Hoerr**[1]

Let's continue to develop the model by examining the characteristics of successful learning spaces, whether they are physical or virtual, that support design thinking. Here is my top five:

---

1 Thomas R. Hoerr, "Decluttering the Teacher-Centric Classroom," Thomasrhoerr.com blog, August 1, 2021, thomasrhoerr.com/decluttering-the-teacher-centric-classroom/.

HUMAN. Learning spaces should be places that people want to spend time in. Human spaces engender a sense of belonging, safety, and community. These spaces are inclusive, equitable, and accessible, and they provide every learner with the resources required for success.

INVITING. Learning spaces should be welcoming and invite students into an irresistible experience that inspires wonder and curiosity. Spaces that are inviting communicate that they are places of learning that showcase student achievement and the value of each student.

FLEXIBLE AND AGILE. Learning spaces should be flexible (capable of rearrangement) and agile (they can be transformed quickly). These spaces can be responsive to the requirements of the needs of teachers and students in the moment. Flexible and agile spaces also enable students to shape the space according to their needs, promoting choice and ownership of the space.

CONNECTIVE. Learning spaces should support the development of the relationships that are necessary to support teaching and learning. Spaces that are connective support the spontaneous and unexpected interactions that are essential for creative thought and action. They should also offer access to resources and ideas and utilize technology to support synchronous and asynchronous interactions.

EMPOWERING. Everyone has that space that they enjoy being in and that helps them be productive and creative. A classroom with the right design can become an environment that energizes and inspires students to do their very best. A great design can also enable students to make choices in how they use the space according to their needs.

CREATING LEARNING SPACES FOR DESIGN THINKING

I encourage you to use the design thinking process to understand your specific context for developing your physical and virtual learning spaces.

As you might expect, the redesign of learning spaces can be expensive, and you might not have the authority to make changes to your space, either physical or virtual. However, there are simple and low-cost strategies that you can use to support the creation of a physical/virtual design studio.

> To get a feel for redesigning a physical classroom, watch the three-part Remake Your Class series, developed by The Third Teacher+ and produced by Edutopia. The videos give a great overview of the design process and how it was used to remake a traditional space into a dynamic learning space on a limited budget. The strategies in the video could also be applied to a virtual space. The links to these videos are on the book's website.
>
> **davidjakesdesigns.com/educatordesigner**

Getting Started: Begin with a Learning Space Inventory

As part of a discovery approach to improving your spaces, conduct an inventory of the elements of your physical and virtual spaces. The goal is to establish a baseline understanding of what is available to be used as part of a redesign process. An inventory will also be useful in helping you understand what you don't have that you need.

> I have developed a checklist based on the characteristics of a design thinking classroom that you can download to inform the inventory process. Find it on the book's website.
>
> **davidjakesdesigns.com/educatordesigner**

I recommend using an ERIC grid to gather feedback from your students about your learning space. A radar chart is also a very helpful tool for evaluating spaces. To use this, have evaluators judge each element listed on the chart across a scale of 0 (low) to 6 (high). Here is an example.

Elements of Successful Learning Spaces
I'm evaluating the _____

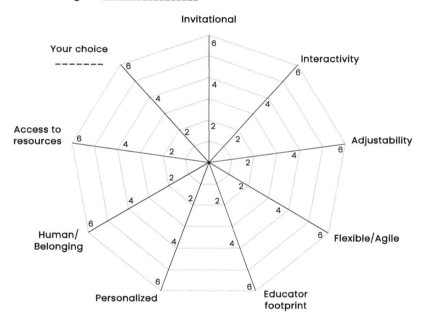

For the physical space, you can also use a sticky note approach, which is both fun and informative. Provide students with four colors of notes to reflect the ERIC categories. But this time, instead of the paper grid, have the students stick the notes on the room itself! This is a unique and fun activity that students like, and it has the additional benefit of casting students as designers. Trust me, you'll get great information.

Let's examine specific recommendations for physical and virtual spaces that you can use to create a design studio.

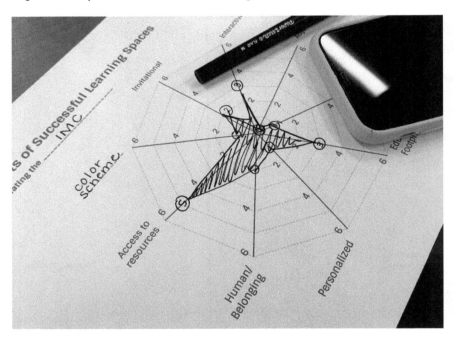

STRATEGIES FOR CREATING THE DESIGN STUDIO: THE PHYSICAL SPACE

Here are seven strategies for transforming your classroom into a space that can support a design thinking experience:

DECLUTTER. Almost every classroom I visit has walls that are filled with posters, pictures, and every artifact possible. There is a growing body of research that suggests that overstimulation created by the physical classroom itself impairs cognitive function and impedes processing and critical thinking. Rodrigues and Pandeirada found that students that performed learning tasks in a visually distracting environment exhibited reduced cognitive function.[2] Similarly, other researchers have found that overstimulating environments promote distractibility and off-task behavior.[3]

You can address overstimulation by rethinking the purpose of the walls of your space. Walls with whiteboard panels installed on them make terrific surfaces for collaborative ideation. Walls can also be used for storage and the display of learning artifacts and student accomplishments.

To declutter your walls, as well as your classroom, remove things from your space that you no longer use. As every teacher knows, this is easier said than done! But you can use the same sticky note technique (using two colors, one for keep and one for discard) to help you analyze your space. Alternatively, completely move everything into the hallway and then add elements that you absolutely need back into the space. This process can be done in conjunction with cleaning and painting the space.

ADD COLOR. It seems that every classroom, and every hallway, in every school is some type of light beige. To be honest, it's time to go beyond beige to add some color to learning spaces. This can be done in a variety of ways: repainting walls, adding colorful furniture, or even adding colorful storage containers. The objective is to use color to add visual diversity to the space, and in the process, create a more engaging and welcoming space.

When adding color to a space, it's important to consider how color influences human behavior. It's also important to consider the cultural connotations of color. One of the first things I do when creating a presentation for an audience outside of the United States is to understand

2 Pedro F. S. Rodrigues and Josefa N. S. Pandeirada, "When Visual Stimulation of the Surrounding Environment Affects Children's Cognitive Performance," *Journal of Experimental Child Psychology* 176 (December 2018): 140–49, doi.org/10.1016/j.jecp.2018.07.014.

3 Anna V. Fisher, Karrie E. Godwin, and Howard Seltman, "Visual Environment, Attention Allocation, and Learning in Young Children: When Too much of a Good Thing May Be Bad," May 21, 2014, doi.org/10.1177/0956797614533801.

how the audience may respond to specific colors. The same consideration is important when designing learning spaces.

A final consideration about color focuses on the age and development stage of the student. Primary-age students favor bright, warm colors (primary colors), whereas secondary students favor "deeper, cooler colors."[4]

An easy way to get started is to repaint a single wall in your classroom space to create an accent wall. Generally, a medium blue or green is a great color choice, as these seem to be universally accepted as two colors that resonate with people.[5] Green is associated with the natural environment and promotes harmony, balance, and collaboration. Blue promotes a calm and contemplative environment and focused study. Other colors, such as red, are generally distracting when placed on a large wall surface, but accent pieces in the room (such as storage bins) can add splashes of color that inspire energy and passion.[6]

ADD WHITEBOARDS. Perhaps the most frequent comment I get from teachers and students about new classroom spaces is the value of whiteboard surfaces. Being able to write, sketch, and problem-solve on any combination of whiteboard walls, desks, and tablets contributes a great deal to the classroom experience. I can attest to that: When I worked at the design firm, everything was writable, from the desks to the walls and the pillars in the studio. The space we worked in was literally a canvas for ideation. Creating spaces for design work is dependent upon having surfaces for ideation and expression. You can dramatically improve

---

4 Vincent J. Spencer and Chelsea Harrell, "Color in the Classroom: Creating Welcoming, Age-Appropriate Learning Environments," lsp3.com, accessed March 22, 2022, ls3p. com/portfolio/color-in-the-classroom-creating-welcoming-age-appropriate-learning-environments/.

5 Haworth, "The Psychology of Color: How Your Palette Influences Workspace Design," Spark Blog, November 27, 2019, haworth.com/na/en/spark/articles/2019/the-psychology-of-color. html.

6 "Create: Colour Special," Spaceoasis, accessed March 22, 2022, spaceoasis.com/wp-content/uploads/2019/06/CREATE-Colour-Special.pdf.

the ability to ideate, prototype, and catalyze creativity by including this capacity in your design-studio classroom.

Unfortunately, commercial whiteboard surfaces are expensive. However, it is easy to convert your existing space with readily available paint that converts any surface into a writable one. You can also visit a hardware store to purchase sheets of inexpensive 4' × 8' whiteboard panels (often called shower board) that they will cut into any size for you. These are also suitable for mounting on a wall. Finally, the book *Make Space* contains a great recommendation for building mobile whiteboards out of a whiteboard panel and a dry cleaning Z-rack.[7] It's terrific and inexpensive.

To get the most recent and updated recommendations for whiteboard paint and surface, as well as instructions for building the Z-rack whiteboard, visit the materials section of the book's website.

davidjakesdesigns.com/educatordesigner

PROVIDE DESIGN THINKING RESOURCES. Students working and learning in a design studio should have access to a wide variety of materials, tools, and storage. This includes simple materials that can be used in the prototyping process. Make sure students have access to a variety of paper types and sizes, including large roll paper. Supply markers, sticky notes, and other office supplies. Slat-wall panels can turn a wall into a place where students can store ongoing work. This also supports the invitation into the space and provides students with the creative inspiration that can come from viewing the work of other students. Finally, if your space is large enough, consider stocking large pieces of foam board that students can use as a project space. Students can tack

---

7 Scott Witthoft and Scott Doorley, "Make Space," Stanford d.school, accessed March 21, 2022, dschool.stanford.edu/resources/make-space-excerpts.

drawings, sketches, and notes onto the board to create a mobile project space that can be used anywhere in the studio.

RETHINK THE TEACHER SPACE. Most classrooms in the United States are between seven hundred and eight hundred square feet with between twenty-five and thirty students. It's been my experience that teachers generally take up to about one-third of this space. Perhaps there is an opportunity to rethink the teacher footprint.

If you have another location to carry out your professional duties beyond teaching other than the classroom (for example a departmental office), consider removing the traditional teacher desk to reclaim that space for other purposes. Use this reclaimed space to create an area for teacher-to-student conferencing or for peer collaboration. You might also create a respite zone, which could feature soft seating and device-charging capacity so that students can recharge mentally while recharging their devices.

CREATE MULTIPLE LEARNING ZONES. In any classroom, there are opportunities to use the space in new ways. As part of a redesign process, visit an elementary school classroom (if you work in a high school or middle school) to see how they create zones for learning. In your space(s), think about the main floor of the space and how it could be recreated to support different learning conditions. How would a reimagined space support direct instruction, collaboration, ideation, reflection, creation, and presentations, all in one location that shifts to meet teaching and learning needs? How could a space be a theater for presentations one moment, a place for storytelling the next, a place for discussion and dialogue after that, and then a center for collaboration? If you have furniture that is difficult to move, what arrangement best fits a design thinking approach? (Hint: collaborative!) Based on your expectations for teaching and learning through a design approach, what zones would you create to form the design studio?

Here is an example of zoning from one of my classroom-design projects.

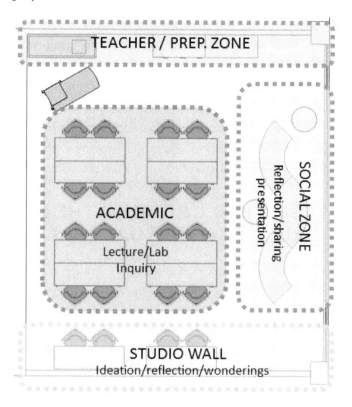

USE THE PERIMETER OF THE CLASSROOM. I have observed that the perimeter is generally the least functional and useful space in a classroom. Except for a whiteboard installation at the front of the space, classroom perimeters are basically used for storage. Instead, enlist the help of school maintenance to build a counter along a wall to create a standing-height café counter. Make it wide enough to be able to set a computer on. Make it writable by using a whiteboard surface to create a design counter complete with ideation capability that provides students with the opportunity to stand and move while engaging in design activities.

WHAT NOT TO DO! If you are going to focus on improving your spaces, there are things that you should not do. Avoid the garage sale! Don't bring that old couch into the classroom—it's a fire, smoke, and hygiene nightmare. Avoid living room lamps, dorm-room refrigerators, and microwaves, which are not designed for the school environment and add to your school's electricity bill in a big way. Avoid furniture from big-box stores; it's not school rated (for fire and smoke release). Avoid adding drapes and other materials into your classroom that might become a fire hazard. Be careful with tall (and large) storage cabinets that are not designed for schools and might become a tipping hazard. Most importantly, ask permission before you start hacking a classroom!

STRATEGIES FOR CREATING THE DESIGN STUDIO: THE VIRTUAL SPACE

At the start of the pandemic in 2020, schools, teachers, parents, and students were thrust into the condition of "remote learning." It was a reactive but necessary response. It's safe to say that the experience of remote learning was challenging for everyone concerned and generally poorly received. There were many probable causes of this, but most were based upon a lack of preparation for teaching online, which is different from using technology face to face in a physical environment. In any case, the experience of remote teaching and learning should have still demonstrated to schools the potential of virtual learning environments. There is no doubt that the future of school includes virtual learning environments.

As a design freelancer, I conduct my work activities in many different locations, including virtual environments. During the pandemic, I experienced challenges similar to those faced by educators when I moved my practice online. Although it was neither easy nor effective at the start, conducting virtual design experiences with my clients is now part of my reality. Working in this way is here to stay.

And I'm obviously not alone. This new reality applies to how the business world will now conduct work moving forward. Businesses have found that people are productive working virtually, spending less time in meetings, and finding more time to do work that they personally consider valuable.[8] However, a key to moving forward with an effective hybrid business environment is matching the task or need to the ability of the virtual environment to support it.[9] This will hold true for education as well, and finding the balance between face-to-face and virtual learning experiences will be crucial to the success of hybrid learning experiences.

"How can we begin to move past an educational model that is tethered to time and place and move closer to learning that is immersive, mobile, collaborative, and social?"

—Educause[10]

Preparing students to be effective contributors in a hybrid work world must become part of what schools do. Having students address real questions through design thinking experiences that take place in a hybrid learning environment is a great start to realizing this.

The model provided in this chapter describes a spatial ecology that reflects a realistic approach for the development of a hybrid physical-and-virtual learning experience. The tools to build this model out may be different from school to school, but the model provides a foundation for a contemporary hybrid learning space that will serve

---

8 Julian Birkinshaw, Jordan Cohen, and Pawel Stach, "Research: Knowledge Workers Are More Productive from Home," Harvard Business Review Performance Indicators, August 31, 2020, hbr.org/2020/08/research-knowledge-workers-are-more-productive-from-home.

9 Susand Lund, Anu Madgavkar, James Manyika, and Sven Smit, "What's Next for Remote Work: An Analysis of 2,000 Tasks, 800 Jobs, and Nine Countries," Mckinsey Global Institute, mckinsey.com/featured-insights/future-of-work/whats-next-for-remote-work-an-analysis-of-2000-tasks-800-jobs-and-nine-countries.

10 "ELI Annual Meeting 2010," Educause, accessed March 25, 2022, events.educause.edu/eli/annual-meeting/2010.

you and your students effectively. Let's examine the role and design considerations of a virtual space.

The Role of the Virtual Space: Success for a Blended or Remote Design Thinking Experience

It is time to recognize the affordances of virtual spaces and how they can be used to create mission-critical locations for learning, including those that support a hybrid or remote learning experience. That means valuing virtual spaces as much as physical spaces.

That's a considerable jump for most schools, administrators, and teachers. And it means developing a continual and committed investment in the infrastructure, support, and professional learning required to make a virtual space both a reliable and value-added proposition for teachers and students.

Let's explore how a virtual design studio can contribute to a design thinking experience.

VIRTUAL SPACES ARE CONNECTIVE. Potential collaborators are everywhere. The use of technology can expand the design thinking experience by enabling students to engage stakeholders remotely. As you might expect, as your comfort level with the process grows, design experiences will become more robust, and you might need to extend beyond the school into the community and beyond. Technology provides this access and enables students to develop and implement remote engagements that are essential to the discovery process.

Technology also provides the opportunity to create a design community for the students you teach. Spaces to connect, create, and share ideas should be an essential component of any design thinking practice.

VIRTUAL SPACES ARE PLACES TO CO-CREATE. Digital tools provide creative capacity and are an essential component of a virtual space. The enormous access to primary-source content, imagery, expert voices, and other resources presents educators and their students an opportunity to create (through original work and remixing) compelling digital products. Designers rarely operate independently or in a vacuum; co-creation with the people that they are designing with is the norm. Leverage virtual spaces to support this type of co-creative experience.

VIRTUAL SPACES EXPAND WHEN AND WHERE LEARNING OCCURS. Making virtual spaces available to students 24-7 provides opportunities for them to make choices about when and where to work. Access to these spaces beyond the school only requires a laptop or a phone to make learning and interacting anywhere and anytime a reality. Having access to these spaces on demand also promotes new, asynchronous types of interactions between students and teachers.

VIRTUAL SPACES PROMOTE DISCUSSION AND THE SHARING OF IDEAS. A great option for extending and amplifying the work of the design studio is to use discussion forums. It's always interesting to pose a provocation at the end of a class that can be discussed online in a forum. Conversely, a provocation posted as homework can provide students with an opportunity to contribute ideas to a learning experience for the next day.

As a classroom teacher, it was obvious to me that five or six students carried the classroom discussions that I wanted to have. But providing a space for students to contribute their ideas in multiple ways enables students to contribute in their own way and at the right time. For example, online discussion forums allow students to carefully construct their contribution rather than having to formulate it in the moment, in front of their peers. Also, students who may not have an initial idea may be prompted to contribute based on another student's comment, even if that's only in the form of feedback.

VIRTUAL SPACES SHOWCASE ACCOMPLISHMENT. In today's world, students must have a virtual presence to show off what they think, what their skills are, and what they can create. Providing a virtual space for creation and contribution helps students create digital products that they can share with others, as they'll need examples for college admissions, scholarships, and job applications. Educator-designers can help students craft a digital portfolio in a safe and responsible way.

Design Considerations

Here are some strategies I recommend for the design of a virtual space.

USE A DESIGN APPROACH. Develop a provocation that leads you into a design process to understand what is available and what you need. Be inclusive and include administrators, students, other teachers, and your school's technology team to help develop the virtual space. As part of the design challenge, have students develop a prototype model that can be refined into an actual space.

FOCUS ON EQUITY AND INCLUSION. Using the same design approach, understand what tools your students have and what their home environments are. Understand where they can work beyond school. Additionally, spend time understanding each student's competency with technology. To the best of your ability, be sure that everyone has the access, tools, and knowledge they'll need to engage in an equitable experience.

PROMOTE STUDENT OWNERSHIP. I'm always in favor of encouraging student ownership of the learning experience. Of course, there are limits to this, but technology-based learning environments associated with remote and blended courses require new thinking about interacting and learning together. Take advantage of social media and the other technologies that students use to develop expectations for behavior. Balance student input against the necessities of conducting school in these environments. Let the learners help you develop the expectations for how remote and blended learning can best function for them and for you.

DESIGN FOR THE DEVELOPMENT OF SKILLS AND LEARNING DISPO-SITIONS. Teach your students how to learn online by supporting the development of the skills they need to work in a virtual environment. Teach them how to work asynchronously. Teach them how to leave an appropriate and helpful comment. Help them to understand privacy issues and online etiquette. Make sure they understand how to use the technology that will support the design thinking process and learning experience.

DEVELOP A DIGITAL PEDAGOGY. Avoid directly mapping the instructional methodologies that you use in your physical classroom to a virtual space. Be aware of how virtual environments challenge your established pedagogical practice and how a new context for teaching can change the nature of educating students. To address these things, use the design process to develop a digital pedagogy that recognizes and considers the specific affordances (and challenges) of virtual spaces. What can you add to your instructional toolbox that can add depth to your teaching practices online? How must your current approaches be adapted or altered (improvement) for a different learning environment? What new approaches (innovation) must be developed to successfully engage students and create an appropriate instructional environment for hybrid or remote work?

To get started, make a chart of the teaching strategies you use in physical locations and ideate around how they can be adapted, rethought, or even discarded (use the Start/Stop/Continue three-column discovery tool from Chapter 5). Invest time in prototyping a digital pedagogy, and realize that it will require iteration and testing under live conditions to improve. To jump-start your thinking, look at Harvard University's Project Zero Thinking Routines or the 16 Habits of the Mind to ground your pedagogy in critical thinking and the development of learning skills and dispositions.[11]

---

11 "Project Zero's Thinking Routine Toolbox," Project Zero, accessed March 29, 2022, pz.harvard.edu/thinking-routines; Institute For the Habits of Mind website, accessed March 20, 2022, habitsofmindinstitute.org/.

See the book's website for more online resources.

davidjakesdesigns.com/educatordesigner

Include generative tools for co-creation. Generative tools support creative capacity. To support creativity and co-creation, include tools that provide team collaborative document creation and team discussions. Add virtual whiteboards, graphics creation and editing packages, and image and photo storage. A tool that supports virtual learning and engaging stakeholders remotely will also be essential.

To keep it all organized, you might develop a design thinking component in a learning management system, if your school offers that capacity. Learning management systems provide a simple way for teachers to develop content and provide resources while offering a consistent interface for students across all their courses. It is also important to consider adding project-management software for students to develop project spaces and assign and track team responsibilities and progress.

WHAT NOT TO DO! The first mistake when using technology with students is to assume that they know how to use it. Students certainly know their phones, texting, and various social media tools that seem to change by the day. They are social users of technology. Educators can help them grow their use of technology by helping them to understand technology as a learning tool.

With that said, don't compete with their technology. You'll lose that battle. Get comfortable with students using and finding their own tools that support their learning in their own way. Let them personalize and self-organize their experience on their own terms. And a word of caution: educators should only engage students through school-approved technology resources. Never communicate with students outside of your school or district's approved systems. But let the kids have their spaces. They are going to use their own tools anyway.

CLASSROOM TECHNOLOGY TOOLS TO SUPPORT STUDENT DESIGN WORK

Throughout the process of design, there are opportunities to leverage technology to support the facilitation of the design process. As a former instructional technology coordinator, I take every opportunity to use technology when I engage clients. I consider it one of my strengths.

Here is a set of recommendations for technology use that are organized by the phase of the design process and the activities of the phase.

Since technology tools change rapidly, I will not be making specific tool recommendations here, but you can access an updated list of technology-based ethnography tools on the book's website.

davidjakesdesigns.com/educatordesigner

Ethnography

Audio, photography, and video are the essential tools of the ethnographer. There are a variety of hardware solutions for these categories, but a smartphone or tablet will work well for your students. Additionally, a variety of apps can be used to facilitate recordings.

I have found that the onboard microphones of a smartphone or tablet are sufficient when in proximity to those being recorded but insufficient at distance—for example, when participants are around a big conference table. My recommendation is to invest in good microphones that capture sound effectively. A Bluetooth microphone that connects to a device works very well and allows me to engage an audience in a large space without a reduction in the quality of the recording.

Likewise, for most of the video ethnography that students do, their smartphones should be sufficient. You may wish to consider the purchase of a gimbal stabilizer (think advanced selfie stick) for your class.

These help you make super smooth video as the videographer walks or moves around a space. Also, for interviews, it is essential to have a small smartphone tripod and phone grip that can be positioned for recording. Both are affordable solutions. There are times when students may wish to create higher-end videos to share their progress or the outcome of their design work; in these cases, higher-end cameras and video equipment may be useful.

Managing Project Work

Design work has a lot of moving pieces. Keeping track of dates, project progress and milestones, files, and design team responsibilities are a must. Project-management software provides a single place where your student-designers can access everything they need to stay up on their project work. There are a variety of capable tools online that can be used by students to manage the design process effectively.

Curating Data

When you collect a large volume of information, it needs to go somewhere—and somewhere safe. Information management is critical when it comes to design work. The information that is generated from ethnography needs to be curated—stored and managed—so that it is accessible for use by student design teams. I store all of what I collect in online storage for access anywhere, on any device. I also link all my data folders into my project management tool so that I have everything in one place.

It's also important to help students develop a protocol (folders and file naming conventions) to help them manage data effectively.

Development of Ideas

Ideas mean everything in the design process. While the point of view and design drivers provide a framework for design, ideation launches the creative and divergent part of design. Technology platforms that support individual and collaborative ideation are highly valuable tools. Look for tools like virtual whiteboards that allow people to engage in ideation. Other tools include more sophisticated capabilities that enable free-form ideation with digital sticky notes while also offering structured templates for more targeted work. Be sure to also investigate apps for smartphones that can assist in ideation. I use an app on my iOS devices to capture paper sticky notes during ideation sessions that enables me to digitally rearrange them to organize ideas and see patterns.

Production of Reports

A part of my responsibility as a designer is to report the outcomes of my design work to clients. Students that engage in design work will need to do the same. As you might expect, there are various tools to support this, but I'm going to suggest that any type of document-creation tool that is used should have collaborative writing capabilities and exist in the cloud. It's important for students to write collaboratively (a new skill associated with writing that has developed because of virtual environments) and have that writing environment be cloud based. This will ensure access to a writing environment across devices and promote effective version control when working with multiple authors.

Also, beyond writing, it is important to consider a page-layout tool that gives student-designers the capability to produce professional compositions. These tools generally have report templates that enable users to blend a variety of media to create dynamic and professional reports.

Media Production

In design work, there is a need to create multimedia to communicate progress and outcome. Videos that tell the story of the design process can be created through a variety of software platforms, some cloud based. Helping students understand how to capture media while doing onsite work with a variety of tools, getting that media off of devices and curated, and then using it in a video-production platform to create a composite video is a challenge. Students are used to pointing, shooting, and uploading with their phones. You can help them develop more advanced multimedia composition skills that will support their work in school and beyond.

Essential Technology: The Checklist

Here are the general classes of tools that you want to consider for supporting a design thinking learning experience.

SOFTWARE

Project-management software

Ideation software, such as virtual whiteboards

Document-creation and sharing tools

Photo-sharing tools

Calendaring tools

Graphic and page-layout software

Video-creation tools

Screenshot tools

Video-reflection tools

Discussion forums

Learning-management system (LMS)

HARDWARE

Laptop/Chromebook

Tablets

Video camera for high-end video work

Smartphones with apps

Microphones (including Bluetooth models)

Gimbal stabilizer for smartphones

Tripods and mounts for tablets and smartphones

THE UPSHOT

The future of learning depends on a connective, broad, and contributory experience. Virtual spaces can be aligned with the physical spaces of schools to create a dynamic and contemporary spatial ecology for teaching and learning. There is no doubt that your students will see this type of environment throughout the remainder of their education and when they enter the world beyond school. Providing the experience now and enabling them to develop the skills and dispositions of an educated person capable of learning, working, and interacting in a hybrid world will serve them well.

CHAPTER 8

Embracing the Journey

This book asks you to rethink much of the way you have previously taught. It asks you to embrace a new journey to learn and apply the design thinking process. This journey, perhaps better framed as an expedition, is about finding a new pathway for leading the education of children and young adults. It presents new challenges, as does any journey, and it presents an opportunity to embrace a destination that will be worthy of your efforts.

All journeys have their beginning. This book asks you to act as a designer and put techniques and strategies into play with the expectation of creating a new classroom experience. If you have experience as a classroom teacher, you already have lessons that work for kids. This hard-won knowledge has been acquired over years of teaching and interacting with students daily. When I taught, I had my go-to lessons that I knew would be successful and that I relied on to be effective in helping my students understand science. These lessons were aligned with my beliefs about education and the way I perceived my role as a teacher. It was no different as an administrator: I had my strategies for interacting with teachers that I knew would be successful from experience.

"Make voyages. Attempt them. There's nothing else."

—Tennessee Williams[1]

---

1 Tennessee Williams, *Camino Real* (New York: New Directions, 1970).

In this book, I've asked you to reimagine how you think about education and about your role as an educator. I've asked you to deeply consider a process that will help you increase your ability to leverage the capacities and the opportunities of a connected, resource-rich world. I've asked you to explore what can be imagined and created through the design thinking process. I've challenged you to think of the values and the opportunities of a design-based educational experience grounded in the construct of an educator-designer.

EMBRACING A SHIFT

As you probably know (and have experienced), engaging in a growth process can be difficult. As educators, you are often asked to make a variety of changes in your practice in response to conditions and initiatives in your school, state, or even nation. Shifting how you think as an educator does not occur overnight. In fact, to be effective, I think educators have to be willing to be patient when engaging in a process that is ongoing and reflective.

Here is an honest question: What would it take to make the shift to design thinking-based pedagogy? What would you have to give up? What would you have to improve or create? And what do you believe would be the most significant constraints that you would have to overcome? How would you shift time and resources? How would you—you fill in the blank. To help you identify this shift, try using the You / Constraints / Could Be You ethnography tool described in Chapter 5 to identify your current beliefs, a plausible future for your action, and the constraints that must be negotiated to get there.

Imagine the challenges.

But that's the good work of school. It's work that is worthy of educators.

Here are the shifts that I expect might be in play.

Moving from	Moving to
Learning occurs in school, siloed	Learning is community-based, connected
Teacher	Educator-designer
The school frames the experience for the teacher	The teacher has ownership of experience
Lessons	Experiences
Finite Subjects	Hyperinterdisciplinary questions
Time is structured, defined by school	Time is allocated based on need, defined by learner
Predictable and expected	Open ended, iterative
Prescribed, known	Authentic, organic
Values answers	Values questions
Efficient, comfortable	Messy, serendipitous
Transactional	Transformational
Curriculum is content-based and unit driven	Curriculum is a set of provocations and design challenges
Classroom is the primary location of learning	Learning occurs across a physical-virtual space continuum
Teacher as driver of learning	Student as owner of learning
Students seen as recipients	Students seen as stakeholders
Change/improvement efforts directed at teachers	Change/improvement efforts directed by teachers
Learning measured by traditional assessments, tests, quizzes, etc.	Learning measured by evaluating the products and solutions created through design

EMBRACING UNCERTAINTY

Education has worked within the context of relative predictability for years. For the most part, schools work most efficiently under predictable conditions. But engaging in a growth-and-improvement process and creating conditions for a new identity and reality for your classroom means moving down a path where the outcome is far from certain. There will be bumps in the road, course corrections, interactions, and more testing. And more testing and improving over time.

As a classroom teacher looking to advance the educational experience you offer, you'll need persistence and an unwavering belief in your journey and what it can mean for you and your students. As an educator-designer, you'll have to put things into play and get better at them. Accepting that the first solution, process, or product is not perfect is part of the design process. Rapid iteration is key, so that as you move forward, improvements will lead to a greater assurance that your design efforts are directionally correct. And the feeling and fear of the potential uncertainty of your journey should be reduced. As educators, we know that uncertainty can be a challenging proposition—especially when standing in front of twenty-five or thirty students—but over time, a classroom culture where continual iterative improvement is embraced should reduce this anxiety. A big shift that you'll have to make is to let go of the expectation that everything will be perfect and correct the first time you do something new.

EMBRACING STRATEGIC RISK-TAKING

A methodology for reducing uncertainty in your change process is to engage in strategic risk-taking. The key word in the previous sentence was *strategic*.

Being strategic means putting in place a variety of support structures and interventions that mitigate the challenges of risk-taking. This is a great approach for an education incubator and a team that helps teachers bring their best ideas into reality. It might mean a broader role for your instructional coaches, if your school has such a capacity.

For the most part, I have found teachers are hesitant about taking risks in their classroom. As an educator-designer, it's important to realize that not being successful at something the first time does not mean it's a failure, it simply means that you have learned more about your opportunity and that you are one step closer to success. I think it's important to remember that the process of design is predicated on testing and iterating a prototype to get a viable solution or product.

Coe Leta Stafford, executive design director at IDEO, says: "You don't have to have the perfect answer. Start making, start doing, and then connect with people to make it better."[2]

My final piece of advice on this topic: rely on the process. When I encounter a challenging and complex design question, I have learned to lean on the process for guidance on how to proceed. That is the value of a process, and adopting this mindset is an important element of operating as a strategic educator-designer.

EMBRACE UNLEARNING

All schools and organizations have their way of doing things. It's called culture. As a designer, I'm always interested in understanding the things that people do without even knowing that they are doing them. This leads to one of my favorite questions to ask to any group that I am working with: What things must you *unlearn* to be able to move forward? In other words, what are the beliefs and perspectives that are part of your classroom culture that must be rethought?

The reason I ask is to understand if those routines and rituals are constraints that might prevent moving forward.

---

2 Suzanne Gibbs Howard and Coe Leta Stafford, "Design Thinking AMA with Suz & Coe," Creative Confidence Podcast, Ideo U, https://www.ideou.com/blogs/inspiration/design -thinking-you-asked-we-answered.

What could you unlearn about homework, about grading, and about classroom management? If you choose to undertake the journey to become an educator-designer, you will have to be willing to reconsider the most critical elements of your practice—things like instruction and assessment.

What does it mean to embrace the ownership of the journey?

It begins with the understanding and belief that design thinking will provide the pathway for reshaping the experience that you provide your students.

It means that, as a classroom teacher, advancing the experience you provide is within your reach and that the most powerful thing that you can do as a professional is to seek continual growth and improvement.

It means that every teacher has something that they can improve, regardless of what conditions or mandates they face. It means that design can help you define what you can improve and provide the pathway for that improvement.

> "One's destination is never a place, but a new way of looking at things."
>
> **—Henry Miller**[3]

It means that you have the power to engage in the journey if you have the right mindset, the tools, and the courage to do so.

With that said, it means that you must be fearless and unrelenting. Growth and improvement take time, effort, and a belief that what you're doing is in the best interests of your students' future.

It means understanding that the destination may not be defined or completely known, but that the journey itself is worthwhile and has value.

---

3 Henry Miller, *Big Sur and the Oranges of Hieronymus Bosch* (New York: New Directions, 1957), 25.

It means that the journey can enlarge the imagination and, in the process, serve as a source of inspiration for you and the lives that you touch.

It means that the journey leads us not just to act differently, but to become something completely new.

A FINAL WORD

Thank you for reading this book. I hope that it has given you the opportunity to explore a new pathway for teaching and learning and for the experience of school. At the same time, I hope what I have written has caused you to reflect on your current practice and inspire you to grow as an educator.

There is much work to do to realize a new condition for learning and what the school experience will become. This effort extends to all members of the school community, but it can start with one teacher. Sometimes change begins in the simplest of ways and builds from there.

I believe that there can be a new identity for educators, one that extends past the simple representations of the past to a bold and vibrant future. I believe this is a moment that can give rise to the educator-designer, an educator who bases their practice on a human-centered design thinking approach.

This approach promotes the development of a design-based pedagogy that is centered on students becoming designers themselves. It enables students to explore the questions and challenges that face the world today—the world that they are part of and that they can lead. There is no time other than now to immerse students in the very real need for improving the lives of people, whether that need is local, regional, or global. No matter their age, from the children of elementary schools to the young adults of high school, there is an opportunity to engage, to understand, and to improve the human condition. Design can provide the pathway. You can provide the opportunity.

At the heart of this book is a belief that schools, and the educational process itself, serve to launch the lives of people. There is no greater calling than that. The way schools have done that in the past and the way they do it now has served students well. There is much we have to be proud of as a profession. But there is a new world today, one that is filled with global uncertainty as well as with the unlimited potential of a hyperconnected world. Such conditions demand a thoughtful consideration of past practice and an objective evaluation of today's schools: Do they provide an education that resonates, that is equitable, and prepares *all* students with the abilities to meet the unknown challenges and opportunities of the future?

The fundamental question that all educators must ask is this: Is what I am doing helping students to be ready for their lives in the context of the future? Not for college, not for a job, *but for a life worth living*? Of course, the answer to that question is complex and not the sole responsibility of the classroom teacher or even the school. But schools do have a part to play, as does every educator, and to answer the question honestly takes bravery and humility. The response, whatever it might be, requires conviction and a steadfast belief that there is no greater opportunity, and no greater purpose, than contributing meaning and direction to the lives of children.

Throughout the book, I have presented several roles for the design process. Certainly, there is an opportunity to embrace the design process as part of a pedagogy and to structure learning opportunities for students. And there are opportunities to use the process of design to drive the change necessary to realize a new iteration of your classroom and even a school. It is my hope that you have made the connections between design and learning and between the process and the meaningful change required to create the schools that children need.

So, take your time. But not too much time. Get started. But read the book again. Take a course on design. But use your classroom as a course. Keep learning. But begin by trying.

Put the design approach into play. Try design, and in the spirit of the process, keep trying and get better at it. Let your kids lead the way. Design with them. Understand that it won't be perfect and that it will be messy but that you will learn. But that's what teachers and schools have always done: learn. If I have any other advice for you, it is to be a fearless learner and believe in your kids and their ability to do great things.

As you have progressed through the book, I hope that I have challenged your thinking and helped you to improve your craft. But most of all, I hope that I have inspired you. In my opinion, inspiration is the engine of change. If people are inspired, they can do anything.

I am proud that the book represents my beliefs and the experiences of my career in education and design. My thanks to the many students, colleagues, schools, and organizations that I have had a chance to work with over the years, who were so formative to my professional career and to my life.

Thank you for reading.

References

Anaissie, Tania, Victor Cary, David Clifford, Tom Malarkey, and Susie Wise. "Equity-Centered Design Framework." Stanford d.school. Accessed January 16, 2022. dschool.stanford.edu/resources/equity-centered-design-framework.

Banks, James A., et al. *Learning in and out of School in Diverse Environments*. LIFE Center. 2007. http://life-slc.org/docs/Banks_etal-LIFE-Diversity-Report.pdf.

Berk, Sarabeth. "The 'What's Innovative?' Debate: Try Using First, Best, and Only." Design Gym. April 26, 2021. thedesigngym.com/whats-innovative-debate-try-using-first-best/.

Birkinshaw, Julian, Jordan Cohen, and Pawel Stach. "Research: Knowledge Workers Are More Productive from Home." Harvard Business Review Performance Indicators. August 31, 2020. hbr.org/2020/08/research-knowledge-workers-are-more-productive-from-home.

Carroll, Maureen, and Laura Mcbain. "Where Empathy Meets Learning: Exploring Design Abilities in K–12 Classrooms." *Voices from the Middle* 29, no. 1 (2021): 14–17.

"Cell Division and Cancer." ABPI. Accessed February 1, 2022. abpischools.org.uk/topics/cell-division-and-cancer/cell-division-and-cancer/.

"Create: Colour Special." Spaceoasis. Accessed March 22, 2022. spaceoasis.com/wp-content/uploads/2019/06/CREATE-Colour-Special.pdf.

"Digital Pedagogy: A Guide for Librarians, Faculty, and Students." University of Toronto Library. August 25, 2021. guides.library.utoronto.ca/c.php?g=448614&p=3061959.

"ELI Annual Meeting 2010." Educause. Accessed March 25, 2022. events.educause.edu/eli/annual-meeting/2010.

Field, Kelly. "How PE Teachers Are Tackling 'Physical Learning Loss.'" Hechinger Report. November 8, 2021. hechingerreport .org/how-pe-teachers-are-tackling-physical-learning-loss.

Fisher, Anna V., Karrie E. Godwin, and Howard Seltman, "Visual Environment, Attention Allocation, and Learning in Young Children: When Too much of a Good Thing May Be Bad." May 21, 2014. doi.org/10.1177/0956797614533801.

Gibbs Howard, Suzanne, and Coe Leta Stafford. "Design Thinking AMA with Suz & Coe," Creative Confidence Podcast. Ideo U. https://www.ideou.com/blogs/inspiration/design-thinking-you -asked-we-answered.

Haworth. "The Psychology of Color: How Your Palette Influences Workspace Design." Spark Blog. November 27, 2019. haworth.com/na/en/spark/articles/2019/the-psychology -of-color.html.

Heid, Markham. "Curiosity Is the Secret to a Happy Life." Elemental. February 13, 2020. elemental.medium.com/ curiosity-is-the-secret-to-a-happy-life-3dc5d940d602.

Hoerr, Thomas R. "Decluttering the Teacher-Centric Classroom." Thomasrhoerr.com blog. August 1, 2021, thomasrhoerr.com/ decluttering-the-teacher-centric-classroom/.

Institute For the Habits of Mind website. Accessed March 20, 2022. habitsofmindinstitute.org.

Lund, Susan, Anu Madgavkar, James Manyika, and Sven Smit. "What's Next for Remote Work: An Analysis of 2,000 Tasks, 800 Jobs, and Nine Countries." Mckinsey Global Institute. mckinsey.com/featured-insights/future-of-work/ whats-next-for-remote-work-an-analysis-of-2000-tasks-800 -jobs-and-nine-countries.

Nuthall, Keith, and Becky Perez. "Odyssey STEM Academy: A Conversation with Keith Nuthall and Becky Perez." Education Reimagined. June 17, 2020. https://education-reimagined.org /odyssey-stem-academy-a-conversation-with-keith-nuthall-and -becky-perez/.

"Project Zero's Thinking Routine Toolbox." Project Zero. Accessed March 29, 2022. pz.harvard.edu/thinking-routines.

Rodrigues, Pedro F. S., and Josefa N. S. Pandeirada. "When Visual Stimulation of the Surrounding Environment Affects Children's Cognitive Performance." *Journal of Experimental Child Psychology* 176 (December 2018): 140–49. doi.org/10.1016/j.jecp.2018.07.014.

Setser, Bryan, and Holy Morris. "Building a Culture of Innovation in Higher Education: Design & Practice for Leaders." Educause. April 16, 2015. library.educause.edu/resources/2015/4/building-a-culture-of-innovation-in-higher-education-design-practice-for-leaders.

Spencer, Vincent J., and Chelsea Harrell. "Color in the Classroom: Creating Welcoming, Age-Appropriate Learning Environments." lsp3.com. Accessed March 22, 2022, ls3p.com/portfolio/color-in-the-classroom-creating-welcoming-age-appropriate-learning-environments/.

"What Is Pedagogy? How Does It Influence Our Practice?" Child Australia. Accessed January 14, 2022. childaustralia.org.au/wp-content/uploads/2017/02/CA-Statement-Pedagogy.pdf.

Williams, Tennessee, *Camino Real*. New York: New Directions, 1970.

Witthoft, Scott, and Scott Doorley. "Make Space." Stanford d.school. Accessed March 21, 2022. dschool.stanford.edu/resources/make-space-excerpts.

Woolford, Susan, Margo Sidell, Xia Li, et al., "Changes in Body Mass Index Among Children and Adolescents during the COVID-19 Pandemic," *JAMA* 326, no. 14 (2021): 1434–36, jamanetwork.com/journals/jama/fullarticle/2783690.

Acknowledgments

Any single book is certainly not the effort of any one individual. This is certainly true of this book, as the intent, content, and outcome have been shaped by numerous individuals. The influence of these individuals is wide-ranging, from those that impacted my education to those that supported and encouraged me to become a designer and, of course, to all of my students over the years, who taught me about education, life, and what it meant to be a teacher.

My thanks to Dr. David Wrone, Dr. Bill LeGrande, and Dr. Jack Heaton of the University of Wisconsin–Stevens Point who constantly challenged me intellectually and taught me as a young man about critical thinking, about achievement beyond what I thought I was capable of, and about my place in the world.

I'd also like to extend my thanks to Christian and Le who gave me my start in design at The Third Teacher+ Studio in Chicago. Also, I am deeply indebted to Lori, Emi, Melanie, Teri, Mary, Mike, Jessica, Randy, Kelly, and Jason, who taught me more about design than any degree program could, and who provided guidance and support for learning and applying design. Without these individuals, this book would have been impossible to write.

My thanks to George and Paige Couros for presenting the opportunity to write this book. My appreciation is extended to Salvatore Borriello of the Reading List who stayed with me and the project over the past several years and made this book much better.

Finally, my heartfelt thanks to all of my students over the years, who were formative in helping me to understand the human elements of teaching and of education. Everything that you have read about education in this book comes from them. I am deeply indebted to them for giving me the opportunity to be involved in their lives and to share their wisdom about teaching, learning, and life.

About David Jakes

I always wanted to be a fish biologist. Since my childhood, that was always my career goal. I hold a bachelor's and master's degree in fisheries management and had the good fortune to work as a river biologist for several years in the southeast of the United States.

But as you probably know, life rarely follows an expected and predictable path. That lifetime goal was replaced by the opportunity to become a teacher and to have the honor of teaching over two thousand human beings the subject of biology. During this time, the impact of technology rapidly influenced what happened in schools and in the world, and I had the opportunity to become an instructional technology coordinator for twelve years. My twenty-seven years in education were energizing, frustrating, exciting, and filled with both disappointments and success, generally all at the same time. But I wouldn't have missed that time for anything; those years have meant everything.

Leaving education, I spent several years working at an architecture firm that provided me with the foundation for leading my own design practice. I've had the opportunity to work with clients from around the world, and have seen the world as a result. It's been a great ride and provided me with the opportunity of independence and the ability to shape my life in truly interesting ways, as I saw fit.

Admittedly, I am driven by my work, which is focused on making education a more effective and human profession. It's what I want to accomplish and this book is a part of that. In my spare time, when I am not designing or writing or working, I enjoy traveling, photography, and trying to figure out what is next.

More from

ImpressBooks.org

Empower
What Happens when Students Own Their Learning
by A.J. Juliani and John Spencer

Learner-Centered Innovation
Spark Curiosity, Ignite Passion, and Unleash Genius
by Katie Martin

Unleash Talent
Bringing Out the Best in Yourself and the Learners You Serve
by Kara Knollmeyer

Reclaiming Our Calling
Hold On to the Heart, Mind, and Hope of Education
by Brad Gustafson

Take the L.E.A.P.
Ignite a Culture of Innovation
by Elisabeth Bostwick

Drawn to Teach

An Illustrated Guide to Transforming Your Teaching
written by Josh Stumpenhorst and illustrated by
Trevor Guthke

Math Recess

Playful Learning in an Age of Disruption

by Sunil Singh and Dr. Christopher Brownell

Innovate inside the Box

Empowering Learners Through UDL and Innovator's Mindset

by George Couros and Katie Novak

Personal & Authentic

Designing Learning Experiences That Last a Lifetime

by Thomas C. Murray

Learner-Centered Leadership

A Blueprint for Transformational Change in Learning Communities

by Devin Vodicka

Kids These Days

A Game Plan for (Re)Connecting with Those We Teach, Lead, & Love

by Dr. Jody Carrington

UDL and Blended Learning

Thriving in Flexible Learning Landscapes

by Katie Novak and Catlin Tucker

Teachers These Days

Stories & Strategies for Reconnection

by Dr. Jody Carrington and Laurie McIntosh

Because of a Teacher

Stories of the Past to Inspire the Future of Education

written and curated by George Couros

Because of a Teacher, Volume 2

Stories from the First Years of Teaching

written and curated by George Couros

Evolving Education
Shifting to a Learner-Centered Paradigm
by Katie Martin

Adaptable
How to Create an Adaptable Curriculum and Flexible Learning Experiences That Work in Any Environment
by A.J. Juliani

Lead from Where You Are
Building Intention, Connection, and Direction in Our Schools
by Joe Sanfelippo

Evolving with Gratitude
Small Practices in Learning Communities That Make a Big Difference with Kids, Peers, and the World
by Lainie Rowell

Printed in the USA
CPSIA information can be obtained
at www.ICGtesting.com
LVHW051138230424
778165LV00002B/341